The Challenge of
The Challenge of
Development

The Challenge of
The Challenge of
Development

edited by

A.D. Tillett

**Papers from a Colloquium convened by the
Lester Pearson Institute for International Development
Dalhousie University, Halifax, Nova Scotia, Canada
March 27 & 28, 1992**

We acknowledge with gratitude the financial assistance of the International Development Research Centre (IDRC).

Canadian Cataloguing in Publication Data

Main entry under title:

The Challenge of The Challenge of development

Proceedings of a colloquium dedicated to the examination of the 1991 World development report and held in Halifax, N.S. in March 1992. Includes bibliographical references.

ISBN 0-7703-9488-4

1. World development report (1991) – Congresses.
2. Economic development – Congresses.
I. Tillett, A.
II. Lester Pearson Institute for International Development.

HD82.C52 1993   338.9   C93-098709-8

75877

Publication Management:

Nancy Hayter

Cover design and camera-ready copy:

Hayswin Productions

Printing:

McCurdy Printing and Typesetting Limited

Published by:

**The Lester Pearson Institute for International Development
Dalhousie University, 1321 Edward Street
Halifax, Nova Scotia Canada B3H 3H5**

1993

Table of Contents

Part One

Part Two

Commentaries

List of
Tables, Figures, Appendices

Tables

Figures

Appendices

Preface

The second LPI Colloquium, which was held in March 1992, was dedicated to an examination of "The Challenge of Development", *the World Development Report (1991)*.

The colloquium format is flexible and puts a primacy on discussion and comment rather than formality; it is open, subject to space limitations, to all members of the community interested in development. We were fortunate to count Vinod Thomas, the principal author of the 1991 Report, among our guests. (Perhaps as a note of respect to his august institution, a number of students wrote him a letter of protest (pp. 107-109), which he took in stride.)

This volume contains the revised proceedings of the Colloquium together with an introduction, three commentaries and the letter. Although the papers appear slightly later than intended, I hope that readers will agree that they continue to have value. We hope that they will stimulate discussion and ensure that the Bank's activities receive the critical examination that they surely deserve.

The success of the Colloquium depended on the participation of staff, students and members of the community, all of whom showed that development issues remain an important interest to Canadians. We were stimulated by our visitors: Pierre Beemans (IDRC); Jim Carruthers (CIDA); Don McMaster (CIDA); Ruben Mendez (UNDP); Amitav Rath (PRI, Ottawa); Bob Miller (Parliamentary Centre, Ottawa); and Vinod Thomas (IBRD) who contributed a helpful dose of wisdom and tolerance to the discussions. In addition, Elisabeth Mann

Borgese gave a stimulating speech at the official dinner and Shirley Conover, Rowland Smith and Bob Clarke proved to be firm and prudent chairpersons. Our thanks to them all.

The Colloquium was supported by Dalhousie University and by a grant from the International Development Research Centre (Ottawa). Our thanks to Chris Smart, Acting Director (who unfortunately was unable to be present) and to Melinda Glockling, Program Administrator, both of the Social Sciences Division.

The Colloquium was organized by Barry Lesser, Associate Director of the Lester Pearson Institute and Professor in the Department of Economics, Dalhousie University, and Paul Bowles of St. Mary's University, Halifax. Nancy Hayter, Publications and Special Events Coordinator, undertook the arrangements with her customary skill and care, and has prepared this book for publication and distribution. The manuscript was typed by Bernie Misener who was able to make sense of the changes and revisions. They deserve gratitude for their patience and work.

A.D. Tillett

April 1993

Contributors

Paul Bowles is Professor of Economics at Saint Mary's University in Halifax, Nova Scotia, Canada.

Barry Lesser is Associate Director of the Lester Pearson Institute for International Development and Professor of Economics at Dalhousie University, Halifax, Nova Scotia, Canada.

Ruben Mendez is Chief of the Technical Support Division of the UN Sudano-Sahelian Office in the United Nations Development Programme, United Nations, New York, U.S.A.

Robert Miller is Deputy Director of the Parliamentary Centre in Ottawa, Canada.

Amitav Rath is Vice-President of Policy Research International in Ottawa, Canada.

Vinod Thomas is a Chief Economist for the Asia Region of the World Bank, Washington, U.S.A., and principal author of the World Development Report (1991).

A.D. Tillett is Executive Director of the Lester Pearson Institute for International Development and part-time Professor of Economics at Dalhousie University, Halifax, Nova Scotia, Canada.

Part One

THE CHALLENGE OF
DEVELOPMENT:
AN INTRODUCTION

A.D. Tillett

The *World Development Report 1990 (WDR90)* dealt with poverty. *The World Development Report 1992 (WDR92)* examined environment and development. In between these two, the *World Development Report 1991 (WDR91)* dealt with the theme "the challenge of development" and is primarily concerned with, drawing on development theory and experience of the last thirty years, an identification of the factors that have made for successful, even sustainable, development. By extension, it is the absence of these factors which explain unsuccessful development. Chief amongst these factors is private markets; unsuccessful countries have evidenced an over-reliance on government-led development and an under-reliance on market-led development. This conclusion gives rise to the principal recommendation of *WDR91* which is a call for a so-called "market friendly strategy".

This Report is a critical review of *WDR91*. It may seem, on the surface, to be somewhat out-of-date, *WDR92* having already appeared and *WDR93* being soon to appear. But the theme of *WDR91* and its major conclusion/recommendations continue to make it timely to examine. More importantly, the three Reports from *WDR90* to *WDR92* are a package which in total defines the main planks of the World Bank view of development and development priorities for the foreseeable future. As such, *WDR91* is especially important because there is a very real sense in which, despite its appearance in the middle of this troika of Reports, it is paramount.

Both *WDR90* and *WDR92* go to considerable lengths to try to demonstrate that poverty alleviation and environmental integrity, respectively, are complementary to the goal of greater economic efficiency which is to be realized through a greater reliance on private market forces. If one is to critically assess these arguments, regardless of whether the result is to agree or disagree, it is essential that one have a thorough and proper appreciation/understanding of the market friendly strategy advocated in *WDR91*. And it is through a thorough review of *WDR91* itself that such an appreciation/understanding can be gained. This, then, is the rationale behind this publication which is based on a colloquium on *WDR91* held at Dalhousie University in March 1992.

WDR 1991

The *World Development Report 1991* (*WDR91*) differs from previous World Development Reports because of three qualities: its comprehensive approach; the synthetic nature of its conclusions; and the forceful, not to say didactic, lessons which it is willing to draw for developing countries. These qualities are admirable even if *the Challenge of Development* explains more than it advocates and its advocacy of practice is based on principles which are not empirically verifiable, at least not definitively.

The theme of *WDR91*, "the challenge of development", is as important as the institution that produced and endorsed it. Indeed the two are so closely linked, in the mind of the reader if not in the text itself, that it is difficult not to think of *WDR91* as the official view of the Bank, and one the Bank will use for direct programming. But the relationship is neither so direct nor the equation so simple. *The*

Challenge of Development is critical, in a way that the Directors of the Bank rarely appear to be, of industrial countries and multilateral agencies as well as of developing countries. Part of the appeal of the *WDR* also lies in its ability to make connections between disparate examples, move with ease between macro logic and micro evidence, and provide the reader with a comprehensive view of the world, particularly that part of the world which lacks wealth, security of fundamental rights and diminishing opportunities. The goals of improved welfare and the eradication of poverty, as advocated in the Report, will be shared by most conscientious people. But the method endorsed for accomplishing all of this, a confidence little short of absolute in the market or price mechanism, is the feature of the Report which is indistinguishable from the institution. It is this feature that makes many observers uneasy.

The Challenge of Development seeks to draw lessons for developing countries from the experience of the past two decades, and by doing so, to clarify the factors that have made for successful, perhaps even sustainable, development. The Report, which is based on an impressive, if partial, quantity of evidence, concludes that economies should be "market friendly"; that governments can usefully provide a framework for such activity; and that *complementarity* between market forces and government structures are essential for effective development. The Report explains, in a characteristically vigourous manner, that:

> If markets can work well, and they are allowed to, there can be substantial economic gain. If markets fail, and governments intervene cautiously and judiciously in response, there is a further gain. But if the two are brought together, the evidence suggests that the whole is greater than the sum. When markets and government have worked in harness, the results have been *spectacular*, but when they have worked in opposition, the results have been *disastrous*.[1]

The remainder of *WDR91* seeks to explore this message and adds, for good measure, a coda on the nature of government and the value of institutional change necessary to guarantee results.

Long Term Growth

If we accept for the moment the necessity of balance between government and markets, (while noting that much will depend on definitions), long term growth is conventionally and conveniently illustrated as the rate of change on the level of per capita income; and if a case is to made for the thesis of the Report by examples from particular economies, as it must, then the illustrations are most likely to be found in those economies which have demonstrated strong per capita growth since 1965.[2] At first, it might seem sensible to comprehend the differences by regions, which the Report relies on when discussing total factor productivity. If the world per capita average is the norm, gross domestic product per capita increased by 1.6 percent during the period 1965-89 and East Asia was the only region clearly above the average.[3] However, by examining the complete list of countries, which is reproduced in Appendix 1.1, pp. 24 - 25, it is apparent that there is both greater variety and a greater dispersion in the long term growth experience than regional analysis admits. Table 1.1 attempts to simplify the long term growth experience by taking the growth rate and examining the relative performance between 1965-80 and 1980-89 of industrial (I) and developing (D) economies for production and exports. The figures in the Table refer to the number of countries which achieved specified rates of growth in per capita income, total output and exports. As the Table shows, 34 developing countries reached the world average for per capita income growth and more than 15 obtained per capita rates above 3.2 percent per annum, that is, double the world average for the period 1965-89.

Table 1.1
Long Term Growth Performance (number of countries)

	Per Capita 1965-89		GDP Growth 1965-80		GDP Growth 1980-89		Export Growth 1965-80		Export Growth 1980-89	
World	1.6		4.1		3.1		6.7		4.1	
Per Capita Growth Rates	I	D	I	D	I	D	I	D	I	D
3.2 +	7	15	6	15	4	12	4	6	5	8
1.6-3.1	13	19	5	16	4	10	9	5	8	13
0.0-1.5	1	22	0	15	0	3	0	7	0	5
-1.6-0.0	0	15	-	3	-	2	-	0	-	2
-3.1-1.5	1	5	0	0	0	0	1	1	0	1
Total	22	76	11	49	8	27	14	19	13	29

Source: see Appendix 1.1, pp. 24-25.

The industrial countries tend to be in the upper ranges with one or two exceptions, but the Table demonstrates the superiority of country when compared to regional analysis for long term growth. There are, for example, five African countries, four countries from Europe and the Middle East and one from Latin America (Brazil) in the highest performance group of developing countries, with the remaining five being part of East Asia. However, there were 49 countries with national economic increases over the world norm in the first period and only 27 in the second; export growth rates above the world average of 6.7 percent (1965-80) and 4.1 percent (1980-89) levels were registered by 19 and 29 developing countries respectively. These crude indicators are enough to show the range and variety of the growth experience among developing countries; one would expect *WDR91* to concentrate on these in order to tell us why some countries have grown and others have not, but it does so only selectively. The Report has a card - in its view an ace - to explain why some countries have done well and that is the adoption of a "market friendly approach".

How to be Market Friendly

The Report advocates a "market friendly" strategy (MFS) for development, the main elements of which are to be found in Figure 1.1. The egg-shaped areas are the key ingredients. The exploration of these four "good eggs" are the foundation of the Report.

(a)   Investing in people:

Recognizing that "markets in developing countries cannot generally be relied on to provide people...with adequate education...health care, nutrition and family planning services" (p. 6), the Report examines *health* and *education*, both seen as ends in themselves but with substantial economic benefits. For example, "a one year increase in schooling can augment wages by more than 10 percent after allowing for other factors"[4] as well as the potential to absorb modern technology. Further, education promotes entrepreneurship because of the increased capacity to take risks.[5] Rapid *population* growth is regarded as a threat to the environment and natural resource use, although it is admitted that "population growth may exacerbate other market failures beside the depletion of resources,"[6] such as urban congestion. Slower population growth is seen as an urgent requirement.[7] Governments should promote preventative programs for "family planning, nutrition education and supplementation and perinatal care", although the Report acknowledges that, over time, developing country epidemiological profiles change and will require curative programs.[8] Educational policy should concentrate on expanding primary and secondary education rather than universities;[9] and will encourage equity as well as technological potential. The Report does not advocate an increase in financial resources; rather it advocates that "where public spending is warranted, it needs to be better targeted"[10] and regards the 'policy climate' as key to human resource investment.

Figure 1.1

The Interactions in a
Market-Friendly Strategy for Development

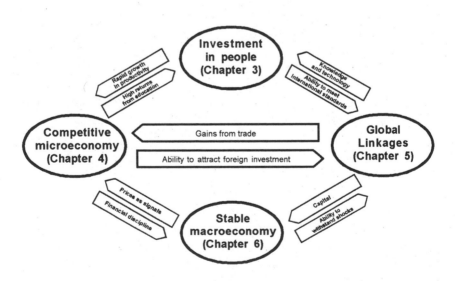

Source: *World Development Report 1991*, "The Challenge of Development", Oxford University Press, 1991, p.6.

(b)   The climate for enterprise:

The second important feature of the MFS is creating an enterprise climate which consists of "the right market signals, the right institutions and the right supportive investments". Indeed the task appears to be neither more nor less than nation building.[11] This argument is based on three examples: *first*, agriculture where increased *real prices* and a reduction of *subsidies* have led to increasing production, based on aggregate supply responses. For this to occur there has to be an integrated policy package of economic incentives (exchange rates, prices, and public expenditures) together with complementary factors (agricultural research and development, extension, credit and marketing services). The Report adds that such services do not necessarily have to be provided by state institutions or government agencies; rather the government should:

> let markets work and (to) facilitate the emergence of private programs, both domestically and externally...(p. 77)

Second, governments should thoroughly revise their industrial and labour *regulations*. In the case of the former, industrial regulations often decrease rather than increase competition and restrictive trade practices limit market growth.[12] Employment regulations, we are told confidently, "can undermine the link between pay and performance and also lead employers to hire fewer permanent workers"[13] and this employment practice is seen as a particular danger for the public service.

Third, when investment projects are measured for *distortions* in trade, foreign exchange, interest rates and fiscal deficits, economic rates of return are consistently higher in undistorted markets and lower in distorted markets.[14] The same studies demonstrate the importance of competent managers, public participation, and a strong infrastructure. In the case of World Bank projects in particular and implicitly in the case of public sector projects in general, the Report draws the following lessons:

> First, it pays to limit public sector investment and institutional support to areas that help foster competition and the

private sector, rather than crowd it out. Second, external aid and lending agencies should promote the involvement of private sector and local communities in decisions about the provision of public services. Third, aid is likely to work much better when used for projects undertaken in competitive and market oriented climates. And finally, external agency support for improvements in policy climate pays off. Perhaps the most powerful rationale for supporting structural reforms is that they raise the productivity of investments - public and private.

(c)   Integration with the World Economy:

The third bundle of the MFS advocates a greater reliance on the world market, particularly world price signals. Global economic integration has three dimensions: technology flows, direct foreign investment and trade. The first, *technology flows*, it is claimed, are encouraged by open economies, particularly if governments are committed to a combination of domestic and international competition, while providing a suitable framework for the use of technology through mechanisms such as information services, norms and standards as well as intellectual property. Research and development is valued although national research laboratories are only tepidly endorsed (p. 92), as the MFS' main purpose is the encouragement of private firms. The second dimension, *direct foreign investment*, provides a channel for technology flows. (The Report has a Table showing that foreign firms are more productive than domestic firms in all of three countries.)[15] It requires policies which reduce distortions and therefore a clear regulatory framework. Direct foreign investment flows, not surprisingly, will depend on bilateral relations [16] The third dimension, *trade policy,* is regarded as the most important mechanism for integration into the world economy; protection leads to price distortions and significant costs for consumers, increasing prices and lowering productivity.[17] Although the Report admits to a number of successful market interventions by governments, in general these actions are regarded as risky and, in consequence, government's influence on trade policy should be limited to encouraging competition, reducing distortions and ensuring that interventions are finite (see p. 101). In summary,

> Openness to trade has improved resource allocation, increased competition and product specialization and provided a broad avenue for technology transfer (p. 108).

(d)   Macroeconomic foundations:

> These are the corset of stabilization and adjustment - shape with flexibility. Developing country governments, in order to encourage both investment and stable expectations, have to revise their fiscal policies in order to bring taxation and expenditure into balance; defeat hyperinflation and reduce 'normal' inflation; and ensure an equilibrium exchange rate. Although there are questions about the speed of the reform, the Report sees macroeconomic stability as a product as well as a result of credibility, encouraging complimentarity between policy goals and leading to higher domestic and foreign investment flows. Private investment flows are reduced by policies that favour the public sector (p. 119), and/or lead to high real interest rates and/or have a heavy debt burden (p. 120). The secret of the macroeconomic foundations lies in the revision in tasks of government and the private sector (p. 8).

State Reform

These four dimensions constitute the core of the MFS. In order to make the policies both explicit and permanent, a fifth dimension is added, namely, state or government reform, which is based on the following principle:

> governments need to do less is those areas where markets work, or can be made to work, reasonably well. Governments need to let domestic and international competition flourish (p. 9).

The Report states that this principle will require a more honest examination of the costs of government economic direction than hitherto, not least a frank admission of the corrupt nature of many vested interests; greater participation leading to a social consensus about the goals of development; and a renewed concentration on equity and distribution principally by ensuring that public funds are targeted to the weak and poor. Further, governments should examine their employment, military, public investment and transfer costs in order to ensure that they are leaner and fitter for development tasks.

The MFS Bundle

The Market Friendly Strategy (MFS) assumes that prices, principally world prices, are the best policy signals. As most developing economies are only slowly inching toward MFS, if at all, Table 1.2 attempts to illustrate its various dimensions in one convenient place. The three columns list first, the constituent elements of MFS; second, the indicators used to describe the sub-elements, and third, the policy aspects. One obvious conclusion from a cursory review of the Table is that the policy implications of a simple idea can be very complex. Because the package is likely to be implemented in different times and places, the Table reinforces the point made previously, of the enormous range and depth of developing country circumstances. One recognizes that *WDR91*, for this reason if no other, hopes to reduce government tasks to a reflection of the market mechanism to allow government, by an agreed consensus, to concentrate on overall policy or the macro-economic framework. In all the sections of the Report - from human resource development to government change - the *leitmotif* is the importance of structural reform, based on a redefinition and reduction of government functions, and in particular the benign climate which arises from the resulting stable macroeconomic framework. But to get to here from there - to cross the road in heavy and speeding traffic - requires not just skill, and perhaps a little luck, but an ability to make effective decisions; that is, it requires greater policy capacity.

Policy Capacity

Policy capacity can be defined, for the purposes of this introduction, as the competence to make effective policy decisions. Policy capacity is that area of national economic practice which permits choices to be made by governments. It lies, as a category, between institutional reform and state reorganization on the one hand, and development outcomes or results on the other. Thus a country like Japan, for example, has policy capacity because it went through the process of structural reform, described in the Report, and has a very successful record of growth and wealth creation.[18]

Table 1.2 - Market-Friendly Elements

MARKET-FRIENDLY ASPECTS	INDICATORS	POLICIES
Investing in People		
Health	Nutrition Life expectancy Adult illness Cause of deaths	Education Non-public delivery Preventative campaigns
Education	Adult literacy Enrolment rates Education & wages	Expand primary & secondary education Technical skills
Population	Environment Urbanization	Family planning
Climate for Enterprise		
Markets	Prices Competition Privatisation	Greater information Reduce distortions Entry/Exit barriers
Institutions	R & D Credit/Subsidies SOE marketing	Regulatory framework Participation
Supportive Investments	Transport Utilities Training	Reduce subsidies Target
Global Integration		
Technology	Trade/Tariffs Technology M Licensing Production costs Norms/Standards Intellectual property	Open economies Diffusion promotion Provide greater information Reduce barriers to competition Labour augmenting
Labour	Intellectual Migration Remittances	Open immigration & migration
Direct Foreign Investment	Net flows Growth	Investment codes Abolish protection Tax neutrality
Trade	Protection Tarriff/Non-tariff Trade growth Commodity prices Trading blocs	World market prices Performance Requirements Export rates Tax reform
Macroeconomic Foundations		
Stability	Current account Fiscal balance Inflation Terms of trade Investment	Fiscal & monetary policy Export growth
Growth	Growth rates Tax & public deficit Real wages Urban & rural poverty	Fiscal reform Currency value & circulation Social impact & policy
Art of Reform	Inflation Devaluation Political crises Comprehensive M liberalizaiton Deregulation	Credibility Stability Timing Speed Scope Sequencing
Investment & Savings	Growth Credit flows Global conditions	Tax incentives

WDR91 discusses the manner by which policy capacity can be strengthened. Governments should act by following three rules: to intervene reluctantly, to apply checks and balances, and to intervene openly, that is, without side deals or negotiations.[19] The government thus becomes an umpire, with policy capacity having the ability to balance interests and settle disputes, and enforce rules which economic agents understand and respond to. With this we have entered a world of rational expectations based on common appetites and desires, which assumes a working, functioning economy over which the solons of government sit. This idea is expanded in the final section of the Report and although, because of numerous examples, it has a greater sense of realism, it remains an elaboration of these three simple guidelines.[20] The Report sees a happy marriage between market-led development and an appropriate policy environment.

> The complimentarity of a sound policy climate and market friendly interventions is one of the most encouraging lessons of development experience.[21]

However, like any fairy tale, there is a dark side to the external world which requires not only the support of developing country governments (and their populations) but other national and international agents; the latter must be willing to co-operate in order for economic rationality to function and suitable development to proceed.

Table 1.3 - Policies for Action

POLICY ACTIONS	Industrial Economies	IFIs	Developing Economies
Trade restrictions	x		
Reform macroeconomic policy	x		
Increase financial support	x	x	
Support policy reform	x	x	
Encourage sustainable growth	x	x	
Invest in people			x
Improve climate for enterprise			x
Open economies			x
Get macroeconomic policy right			x

Even in a Report which advocates reform *tout court*, there is a sensible (and prudent) recognition that structural change in developing countries requires reform in industrial countries and multilateral institutions. These mutual obligations - you restructure and we will reform - are listed in the Report and translated into Table 1.3 with policy requirements shown for industrial countries and multinational institutions, as well as developing countries. Developing countries are, it should be noted, a far less coherent group than the G7 (or the OECD) and the International Financial Institutions (IFIs). Thus, the policy reform process depends not only on the good intentions of governments but on a number of other, and potentially more influential and more cohesive, actors over whom developing countries have little control. So the weight of external to internal factors becomes a crucial consideration in the evolution of policy capability and might even be described as the test by which capability is proven.

All discussants would agree that policy capacity is best judged by results and it is no surprise to find that many poorer countries have, as a combination of luck and judgement, objectively poor records. The counterpoint is to examine those countries which were objectively poor in the past, have prospered and are now wealthy or wealthier than expected. These are, of course, the countries which provide the examples for the global MFS. As a result, the argument often comes down to those who believe the East Asian countries are a special case (or a series of special cases) and so cannot be repeated, and those who argue that their example can or must be repeated in order for developing countries to grow and develop. The Report is clear on the issue; although there may be some differences in world trading conditions from forty or thirty years ago, governments should evolve a policy capacity which mimics, as far as possible, the successful, and from the examples of *WDR91*, East Asian, countries. For development to succeed, governments should accept MFS; for MFS to succeed, governments should develop a policy capacity in three key areas:

(a) Policy capacity and openness:

Although there are many definitions of "openness", smaller economies, (a category which includes the majority of developing economies)[22] are unlikely to be able to pick and choose which aspects of the external world they will use and which they will not. Indeed it is an agreed characteristic of developing countries that they are unable, except in a number of genuinely special cases,[23] to influence world markets. Nevertheless, the Report appears to advocate MFS as a policy whatever the external circumstances,[24] even though countries and the constituent dimensions that make up the MFS differ, and quite sharply, by their susceptibility to external, i.e., world trends. If sensible policy requires a higher than average probability over outcomes, a calculation of the degree of domestic as against external control is a crucial issue.

The Report explicitly recognises the importance of "the climate of development"[25] but by insisting on policy reform as an end in itself, glosses over the implicit *quid pro quo* between domestic and external factors. So developing countries might go through an adjustment process - liberalizing trade and prices - only to find a rapid growth of imports is not compensated by a strong inflow of direct foreign investment on the capital account, and that prosperity is strongly skewed to the wealthy. It is unclear how a strong educational policy, for example, can easily overcome short term financial imbalances which, given the global market, will need to be corrected at once. Again one can agree, for example, that the Uruguay Round of trade reform is an improvement on self-sufficient trading blocs but not that the Uruguay Round is itself able to provide greater opportunities to all, or even a high proportion of, developing countries. If an MFS policy capacity is to succeed it will have to be recognized that a high proportion of decisions are weighted on co-operation with the developed countries (and donor institutions) on *their* terms, and if not on their terms, then in a way which is not necessarily under the control of any national government.

World economic growth will therefore play a crucial role. The World Bank's baseline projection assumes that between 1990 and 2000, the output of OECD member countries will grow at 2.9 percent and world trade will grow by 5.8 percent in real terms; developing countries are estimated to grow by 4.9 percent.[26] Although the Report pays obeisance to the risks inherent in reform, it states that "better domestic policies could raise GDP growth by twice as much as external factors" and at a later point:

> ...an increase of 1 percentage point in the growth of the OECD could raise the developing countries's growth over the long term by 0.7 percent.[27]

External factors, therefore, play an important and more than a facilitating role. Combining these figures, OECD or industrial country growth is estimated to account for 41 percent of developing country growth (i.e. 2.9 x .7) with the remaining 58 percent a result of domestic sources of growth, presumably the result of policy reform.[28] However, by treating all developing countries as a single unit or regional groups, the Report does not come to terms with domestic policy making, nor allow for the implicit and explicit competitions between developing countries for OECD markets. Assuming that all countries can undertake policy reform, it is unlikely that all countries can reap the same benefits; a positive balance of payments for all, for example, is a logical impossibility. Moreover, there is a danger in assuming that all countries have the same capacity to undertake reforms and reap the same beneficial results, not only because developing countries start from different initial conditions, but because larger countries have greater scope to practice policy capacity and to trade off different potential outcomes in a flexible way. The advice may be more valuable for middle income countries, which have a greater range of economic alternatives, than low income countries which, with the exception of China and India,[29] have a smaller scope and greater possibilities of failure. The increased growth and development of low income countries depends on the willingness of OECD countries to play their part and meet their obligations.

(b)   Policy capacity and trade-offs:

At the heart of policy capacity is an ability to make trade-offs, a skill which will be firmly tested if the world economic climate turns from benign to sour.

The Report deals with trade-offs in two ways, first as a *normative* process, which helpfully emphasises the 'art of reform' and places a premium on the credibility of the macro-reform process while favouring rapid over gradual reform, not least because the requirements of "adjustment usually take place in a time of crisis".[30] Although *WDR91* recognizes three successful examples of gradualism (Japan, Korea and Thailand), it argues that it was *because* they took place in strong and stable economies that they prospered, so that "in general, the analytic case for speed is strong". Second, the Report provides *positive* evidence from an evaluation of World Bank projects which purports to show that openness increases the average rate of return on investment from 8 to 10 percent.[31] Openness is calculated on the basis of four indices: the real rate of interest, the fiscal deficit, and foreign exchange and trade restrictions. The published rates of return show the biggest gains when distortions are removed from the foreign exchange premium (moving from a high to low premium permits gains of 9.5, followed by a reduction in trade restrictions (6.9), the fiscal deficit (4.4) and the real interest rate (2.3). The figures suggest that a combination of foreign exchange and trade restrictiveness are the most powerful combination[32] whereas reductions in the fiscal deficit (as a percent of GDP) have their greatest impact when the share of public investment has a range of 6 and 10 percent of GDP. The information is used to show the importance of the *quality* of government decisions, but it fails, because given the data, it cannot, establish which policy variables have the greatest comparative effect. Therefore the issue of trade-offs is subsumed under a general appeal for reform. Perhaps if there is one lesson, it is that policy capacity is best served by attention to exchange rate distortions. However, there must be some skepticism about the sample and the methods since World Bank projects pass through a number of technical and political nets, hence, their probability of success, when compared to non-WB projects, is high.

(c)   Policy capacity and employment:

The case for developing policy capacity with regard to employment should be clear; personal consumer expenditure is the basis of most, if not all, domestic markets and the principle source of savings;[33] without employment and job creation, it is difficult to see how growth or development can be sustained.

Yet the *WDR* does not discuss employment directly even when examining labour mobility, human resource development and wages. The Report's avoidance of labour issues reflects the present data composition of the *World Development Indicators* (produced annually as an Appendix to the *WDR*) which last included a labour or employment series in the 1988 edition.

Labour and employment are treated as a kind of social cushion or residual to other, market friendly, growth processes. Public sector employment regulation, for example, undermines "the link between pay and performance and leads employers to hire fewer permanent workers."[34] Education is linked to wages[35] but not to employment and there is no discussion of the informal sector which possibly will have to absorb - if the recommended human resource development strategies are followed - an increasingly educated population. In general, employment is equated with wages, rather than structure, and there is the impression that wage rates must be kept flexible in order to permit the policies which produce MFS to flourish.

The unwillingness to examine labour and employment is glaring, not to say perverse, when analyzing technology which the *WDR* describes as the principle source of productivity change. Early in the Report we are told:

> The crucial question for the future is whether national and international policies will permit the potential created by technological progress to be exploited.[36]

The employment implications of the argument are avoided. There is a brief recognition that high wage costs stimulate capital intensity and so impair allocation decisions[37] but there is no discussion of the counter-arguments that current technology is essential for export markets as a guarantor of product quality; or the difficulty of obtaining investment credits for second hand machinery; or that capital is strongly associated with long term growth trends only when the relative growth of wages falls below a compressed ceiling.[38] Technology does not necessarily create employment, even when markets grow.

Technology is also, and perhaps increasingly, proprietary and MFS may well encourage this trend; as markets are broadened there is a greater need for protection. Two illustrations will suffice. First, as part of the argument against trade protection, the Report advocates long term trading relationships between buyers and sellers of specific technologies, and yet does not consider the unwillingness of owners to share their technology as against their techniques.[39] Second, there is no discussion of the threat, faced by farmers in developing countries, of a move away from public (and free) techniques - the foundation of the international research and development system for agriculture (see Box 4.1) - to private (and royalty) patent ownership of new technological advances in biotechnology. These and other research results will no longer be a free and public good. The MFS emphasises private returns in a competitive market (and its associated legal instruments) and underestimates the value of public and general diffusion of technological knowledge for employment growth.

Rapid population growth coupled with growing resource costs require greater attention to employment opportunities and their generation. Where market opportunities have not been able to generate employment, governments have relied on an economy of casual opportunities and livelihoods such that the informal sector has grown to become a cushion for other government policies. The result is a wage rate dualism; labour costs define the modern sector and the remaining employment seekers supply the informal sector. The MFS applies to the former, domestically and internationally; only greater policy capacity can assist the latter.

Conclusions

This brief overview describes the Bank's core analysis, as represented in *The Challenge of Development*. The success of the Report is in placing on record the analytic framework which has become part of the Bank's operational behaviour. Bank officials often argue that the ends justify the means and that it is too early for the policies to have been completely successful. However, waiting is rarely a persuasive argument for nations with responsive political systems. It is unclear, because of the limited number of examples, if evidence is not to be generated from a broader base and with a greater sense of the policy capacity of different national units.

Too often MFS is an assertion which excludes inconvenient changes - employment is a case in point - and sees each country as an example of a universal. One does not need, as the following papers show, to fall into the trap (in Dudley Seers' telling phrase) of assuming that "every case is a special case" in order to question the homogeneity assumption of the Report. Internationalization and its associated attributes require comparisons, but one conclusion, confirmed for domestic cases, can well be applied to the world economy: the need for greater regulation and balance or fairness, particularly between developing and developed countries. Whatever its intentions, the Report leaves the impression that the foundation for economic change is domestic rather than international, and it follows that the principle responsibility lies, in almost all cases, with the developing country. MFS is, however, a package which calls on industrial countries to restructure - as uncomfortable as this may be - and to permit greater access for developing country goods and services; MFS requires a *quid pro quo* to yield results.

The *WDR* is a considerable achievement and provides intellectual basis for many Bank actions. As the Bank remains the most important institution for all developing countries, its views are vital for their, and incidentally our, development policies. The Colloquium and the papers that follow are intended to continue a debate whose importance cannot be underestimated.

NOTES

[1] *The Challenge of Development, World Development Report (1991)* p. 2, (emphasis added).

[2] The World Development Indicators, an integral part of the Report, only provide per capita income measures for the long period, 1965-89 (see T. 1, p. 204-205), whereas for all other measures, the period is divided into two, (1965-80) and (1980-89) reflecting two different sets of world conditions. Attempts to calculate per capita income for the two periods from the Indicators, without the raw data, can lead to uncertain conclusions.

[3] The averages are SubSaharan Africa (0.3 percent per year), South Asia (1.8) and Latin America and the Caribbean (1.9). No figure is given for Europe, the Middle East and North Africa. The OECD countries had an average annual rate of 2.5 percent (see World Development Indicators, T. 1, p. 205).

[4] Based on evidence of 11 countries at different periods, (Cote d'Ivoire, Ghana, Korea, Indonesia, Peru, Malaysia, Nicaragua, Thailand and France, USA and Spain).

[5] The evidence for this statement is based on surveys of existing entrepreneurs and interestingly, given the general unwillingness to support universities by the Bank, a high percentage of Thai entrepreneurs have degrees; in Malaysia, while admitting that family wealth and ethnicity play an important role, "enterprise size is positively associated with the entrepreneur's years of education," so confusing the causality implicit in the argument.

[6] There is a discussion of the differing private and social costs and benefits of children, which is then linked to the removal of trade barriers and economies of scale (p. 59).

[7] "Studies have found that a doubling of government expenditures per capita on family planning programs in urban areas would reduce infant mortality in Colombia and that a twenty percent rise in the proportion of villages with a family planning clinic would reduce infant mortality by more than 4 percent in India" (p. 60).

[8] See p. 62.

[9] "Governments will need to be more selective in choosing which level of education or training to improve, which costs to meet...and whom to subsidize" (p. 64).

[10] See p. 66 with the paragraph continuing "Government spending is not always efficient or equitable."

[11] "Markets for goods, inputs, labour and capital need to be better integrated; from the farm to the town, from the city to the market abroad" (p. 70).

[12] "Internal and external restrictions often exist side by side, compounding each other's adverse effects on technological progress and industrial productivity" (p. 79).

[13] Although fewer "permanent workers" would, in the logic of this Report be a benefit, providing they were infinitely flexible at the micro level.

[14] See T. 4.2, p. 82.

[15] See T. 5.1 which compares firms in the Cote d'Ivoire, Venezuela and Morocco, using relative output per worker and net foreign exchange earnings (foreign sales/X-M). The figures are presented as percentages and appear to show that first there is small output increase in majority owned foreign firms in all countries while domestic firms export more.

[16] "The extent to which direct flows contribute to growth depends largely on the effectiveness of host country policies. The scope for increased inflows of DFI to developing countries will also be determined by industrial country policies" (p. 97).

[17] "...there is a general statistical association between less intervention and lower price distortions on the one hand and higher productivity growth on the other" (p. 99).

[18] See Box 2.2 "What's behind the Japanese economic miracle?" and the use made of Japan as an example throughout the text.

[19] See p. 5 for these useful rules.

[20] See Box 8.1 entitled "For policymakers everywhere; seven lessons in reform" (p. 152), which deals with ownership, policy flipflops, institutional requirements, macroeconomic stability, vulnerable people, the failure of partial attempts, and realism.

[21] *WDR*, p. 5.

[22] Measured by either population or the size of the economy.

[23] Where they have a monopoly or near monopoly of a natural resource or commodity.

[24] "This Report will show that what matters most for any country's economic development is its *own* approach to economic policies and institutions" (p. 12); and for example, pp. 45/46: "... developing countries should not slow their reform efforts simply because of rising protection in industrial ones" (p. 105).

[25] See Box 1.3 where the climate of development consists of the following dimensions: world trade, capital flows, world finance, industrial policy, security, technology, energy and the environment (p. 22).

[26] See pp. 27 and 30. East Asian economic output is expected to grow by 7.2 percent during the decade.

[27] And continues, "Conversely, a 1 percent increase in LIBOR could reduce growth by 0.2 percentage point. A 1 percent increase in the growth of OECD is also estimated to lead to a 0.2 percent increase in exports from developing countries" (p. 123).

[28] On the basis of 40 case studies, the *WDR* claims that "better domestic policies could raise GDP growth by twice as much as better external factors" (p. 30).

[29] See Appendix 1.1 for the overwhelming impact of these countries.

[30] The art of reform consists of credibility, macroeconomic stability, timing, speed, scope, and sequencing, see pp. 116-118.

[31] Based on post project evaluations of 1,200 projects in 58 developing countries which were undertaken between 1960 and 1978/79, see p. 162.

[32] "...when included along the parallel premiums and trade restrictiveness variables, the real interest rate variable loses all economic and statistical significance" (p. 162).

[33] "The larger the fraction of income received by workers at the peak of their earnings, the higher the overall savings rate" *(WDR91*, p. 121).

[34] See p. 80 f.

[35] See p. 57.

[36] See p. 2.

[37] See the discussion of the overcapitalized textile industry of the Cote d'Ivoire.

[38] The total factor productivity calculations show that labour makes its greatest long term contribution to growth when the proportion of capital is greatest. For example, when labour contributes more than 20 percent to growth, 1973-87, there is negative total factor productivity. Education is treated as a separate input from labour (or wages) in the growth accounting scheme.

[39] There is evidence (p. 96) that there is little close association between DFI and technology; while private gains from innovation are crucial to any part of investment package (p. 98).

Appendix 1.1

Developing Countries - Economic Growth and Exports, 1965-89

WB No.	Country	Per capita Growth	Pop. (mn) 1990	Production Growth (1)	Production Growth (2)	Exports (1)	Exports (2)
	World	1.6		4.1	3.1	6.7	4.1
68	Botswana	8.5	1.2	13.9	11.3	-	-
95	Oman	6.4	1.5	13.0	12.8	-	-
21	China	5.7	1,113.9	6.9	9.7	-	11.5
32	Lesotho	5.0	1.7	6.8	3.7	-	-
33	Indonesia	4.4	178.2	7.0	5.3	9.6	2.4
64	Thailand	4.2	55.4	7.3	7.0	8.6	12.8
44	Egypt	4.2	51.0	7.3	5.4	-0.1	9.2
77	Malaysia	4.0	17.4	6.3	2.8	4.6	9.8
94	Korea	4.0	42.4	9.9	9.7	27.2	13.8
10	Burundi	3.6	5.3	7.1	4.3	-	2.6
85	Brazil	3.5	147.3	9.0	3.0	9.3	5.6
66	Tunisia	3.3	8.0	6.5	3.4	10.8	4.1
55	Congo	3.3	2.2	6.2	3.9	10.3	6.2
57	Cameroon	3.2	11.6	5.1	3.2	4.9	-3.3
88	Yugoslavia	3.2	23.7	6.1	1.3	5.6	0.4
56	Syria	3.1	12.1	9.1	1.6	11.4	5.7
31	Sri Lanka	3.0	16.8	4.0	4.0	0.2	6.7
59	Ecuador	3.0	10.3	8.8	1.9	15.1	5.0
61	Paraguay	3.0	4.2	7.0	2.2	6.5	7.0
75	Mexico	3.0	84.6	6.5	0.7	7.7	3.7
74	Mauritius	3.0	1.1	5.2	5.7	3.1	10.5
93	Portugal	3.0	10.3	5.3	2.5	3.4	11.7
97	Greece	2.9	10.0	5.8	1.6	11.9	4.1
67	Turkey	2.6	55.0	6.2	5.1	5.5	11.4
24	Pakistan	2.5	109.9	5.2	6.4	-1.8	8.5
50	Dominican R.	2.5	7.0	8.0	2.4	0.3	1.2
78	Algeria	2.5	24.4	-	3.5	1.8	2.9
63	Colombia	2.3	32.3	5.7	3.5	1.4	9.8
51	Morocco	2.3	24.5	5.7	4.1	3.7	5.7
23	Kenya	2.0	23.5	6.8	4.1	3.9	1.6
20	India	1.8	832.5	3.6	5.3	3.0	5.8
16	Mali	1.7	8.2	4.2	3.8	9.5	5.6
48	Philippines	1.6	60.0	5.9	0.7	4.6	1.3
70	Panama	1.6	2.4	5.5	0.5	-5.7	0.1

WB No.	Country	Per capita Growth	Pop. (mn) 1990	Production Growth (1)	Production Growth (2)	Exports (1)	Exports (2)
18	Burkina Faso	1.4	8.8		5.0	3.6	0.8
72	Costa Rica	1.4	2.7	6.3	2.8	7.0	3.1
19	Rwanda	1.2	6.9	4.9	1.5	7.9	-0.8
47	Zimbabwe	1.2	9.5	5.0	2.7	-	3.8
87	Uruguay	1.2	3.1	2.4	0.1	4.6	2.8
7	Malawi	1.0	8.2	5.5	2.7	5.1	2.9
54	Guatemala	0.9	8.9	5.9	0.4	4.8	-11.7
89	Gabon	0.9	1.1	9.5	1.2	8.6	-0.2
49	Cote d'Ivoire	0.8	11.7	6.8	1.2	5.5	3.1
84	South Africa	0.8	35.0	4.1	1.5	7.8	-8.0
8	Nepal	0.6	18.4	1.9	4.6	-	11.2
53	Honduras	0.6	5.0	5.0	2.3	3.1	2.1
90	Iran	0.5	53.3	6.1	2.4	-	21.6
5	Bangladesh	0.4	110.7	2.5	3.5	-	7.6
91	Trinidad	0.4	1.3	5.0	-5.5	-5.5	-5.1
22	Haiti	0.3	6.4	2.9	0.5	5.5	-6.9
4	Somalia	0.3	6.1	3.5	3.0	4.4	-4.6
71	Chile	0.3	13.0	1.9	2.7	8.0	4.9
11	Sierra Leone	0.2	4.0	2.7	0.6	-2.4	-2.5
13	Nigeria	0.2	113.8	6.1	-0.4	11.1	-2.3
52	Papua N.G.	0.2	3.8	4.1	2.1	14.1	6.4
28	Togo	0.0	3.5	4.3	1.4	-	3.1
2	Ethiopia	-0.1	49.5	2.7	1.4	-0.5	0.4
3	Tanzania	-0.1	23.8	3.9	2.6	-4.2	-8.2
25	Benin	-0.1	4.6	2.2	1.8	-	-
76	Argentina	-0.1	31.9	3.4	-0.3	4.7	0.8
83	Venezuela	-0.1	19.2	3.7	1.0	-9.5	11.3
58	Peru	-0.2	21.2	3.9	0.4	1.6	0.4
96	Libya	-0.3	4.4	4.2	-	-	-
62	El Salvador	-0.4	5.1	4.3	0.6	1.0	-1.6
26	Ctl. African R.	-0.5	3.0	2.8	1.4	-1.3	-3.7
34	Mauritania	-0.5	1.9	2.1	1.4	4.0	3.4
45	Senegal	-0.7	7.2	2.1	3.1	2.6	2.5
43	Bolivia	-0.8	7.1	4.4	-0.9	2.7	-0.8
9	Chad	-1.2	5.5	0.1	6.5	-	-
65	Jamaica	-1.3	2.4	1.4	1.2	-0.4	-2.1
27	Ghana	-1.5	14.4	1.3	2.8	-2.6	5.6
12	Madagascar	-1.9	11.3	1.6	0.8	0.6	-2.2
15	Zaire	-2.0	34.5	1.8	1.9	-	0.6
29	Zambia	-2.0	7.8	2.0	0.8	-0.7	-3.2
17	Niger	-2.4	7.4	0.3	-1.6	12.8	-3.8
14	Uganda	-2.8	16.8	0.6	2.5	-2.9	4.3

Notes: 1) 1965-80; 2) 1980-89. Source: World Development Report, (1989).

LESSONS OF DEVELOPMENT

Vinod Thomas

In the midst of a global recession, it may not be evident that the business of economic development is working, but consider the following. Average incomes in developing countries have doubled over the past three decades, increasing faster than in the United Kingdom, the United States, or Japan during growth spurts. People in developing countries now live some 10 years longer on average than in 1960 - twice the gain the United States could achieve by eliminating both cancer and heart disease. The rate of infant deaths has been nearly halved, child death rates have plummeted, and immunization rates have soared.

Economic growth has been most remarkable in East Asia, where economies, such as Hong Kong, Korea, Singapore and Taiwan, have seen living standards rise more than fivefold in a generation. Averages in human development have been striking in a wider range of countries. Costa Rica and China, for example, have witnessed a stunning increase of over 20 years in average life expectancy. In Chile or Thailand where in 1960, 100 out of every 1,000 infants born did not survive to age one, the lives of 75 of those 100 infants are being saved today thanks to improvements in income and health technology.

Having noted these achievements, however, we must also emphasize that development is not working everywhere. The impressive average performance of the developing world conceals tremendous diversity. In contrast to the dramatic growth record in the East Asian economies, living standards have fallen or hardly improved in three dozen countries with a total population of nearly half a billion people. And average incomes across the continents in the developing world have diverged - precisely the opposite of what has been happening among industrial countries. Asia's average income increased from 15% of the OECD's to 28% in 1989 (Table 2.1). But Africa's declined from 11% of the OECD in 1950 to 5% in 1989, and Latin America's from 52% to 31%.

Table 2.1 - Historical Trends in GDP Per Capita

Region or Group	1830	1913	1950	1973	1989	Growth Rate 1913-50	Growth Rate 1950-89
Asia	375 (40)	510 (23)	487 (15)	1,215 (16)	2,812 (28)	-0.1	3.6
Latin America	--	1,092 (49)	1,729 (52)	2,969 (40)	3,164 (31)	1.2	1.2
Sub-Saharan Africa	--	--	348 (11)	558 (8)	513 (5)	--	0.8
Europe, Middle East and North America	--	--	940 (29)	2,017 (27)	2,576 (26)	--	2.0
Eastern Europe	600 (84)	1,263 (57)	2,128 (65)	4,658 (63)	5,618 (56)	1.4	2.0
Developing Economies	--	701 (32)	830 (25)	1,599 (22)	2,796 (28)	--	2.7
OECD Members	935	2,220	3,298	7,396	10,10	1.1	2.3

Note: Data presented are simple averages of GDP per capita. Numbers in parentheses are regional GDP per capita as a percentage of GDP in OECD economies. Regional groupings include only non-high-income countries. Hungary is included in Eastern Europe group, not in Europe, Middle East and North Africa.

Sources: For 1830-1965, Maddison, background paper. Data for 1950-85 for Africa and Middle East are based on OECD; data after 1985 are based on growth rates from World Bank data base. Benchmark values are 1980 international dollar estimates from Maddison, background paper, if available; from Summers and Heston 1984, otherwise.

These sharp differences are the logical starting point for any review of the lessons of development. Why has economic performance varied so much in the developing world? What must governments do to quicken the pace of progress? And what must markets be allowed to do for greater success in development? Addressing each of these questions in turn in the next three sections, this paper argues that the key explanation of country performance lies in the respective roles accorded to the state and market - and the effectiveness with which the two interact in the pursuit of development. We turn in the final section to some practical issues for reforming the state and the market.

DETERMINANTS OF ECONOMIC PERFORMANCE

Success in national development is the direct result of national policies and failure cannot be blamed on the external environment or on any physical limits to growth. True, global factors - such as OECD growth rates, international interest rates and trade restrictions - affect the pace of development in the aggregate. But they do not explain why growth rates among developing countries vary so much. Under similar global conditions - favourable of unfavourable - countries have fared very differently because they have behaved very differently.

Lack of external financing is often identified as the reason for poor performance. Undoubtedly, external capital and foreign aid matter for development. But how effectively countries use capital matter even more. An improvement in the productivity of capital as small as two-tenths of one percent produces a gain in output that would have required $100 billion in additional capital at previous levels of productivity. The evidence in *World Development Report 1991* convincingly demonstrates that the productivity of capital use varies systematically across countries, according to their domestic policies and institutions. Consider investment projects financed by the World Bank as an example. The rate of return on projects is much higher in countries that have market-oriented policy regimes.

That means that, for better development performance, countries need to look first to their domestic strategies. But no single consideration fully captures the requirements for success. Rather, the domestic factors that matter the most coalesce into its several clusters of factors, that can be summarized by the four "I"s: investments, incentives, institutions - and interactions among the three.

Supportive Investments

No country has developed without adequate investments in people, especially in their education and health. Such investments were the hallmark of development in Scandinavia, Germany and Japan, just as they were in the later development of the East Asian "tigers". What distinguishes all these countries is the size and the quality of their expenditures on human development.

So we know how important investments in people are, yet in many countries military spending exceeds the combined spending on health and education, which too often, comes to less than 5% of GDP. Spending priorities within the social sectors are also often misplaced. For instance, vast sums of money are spent on a large school or hospital, rather than on teaching materials and vaccines for hundreds of rural primary schools and basic health clinics. In many countries, heavy subsidies are provided for higher education at the expense of spending on primary education, where the social returns are very high.

An efficient domestic economy also requires sound investments in infrastructure. Adequate roads, ports, power and telecommunications ease the way for successful development, as does investment in agricultural irrigation and research, where returns can be exceptionally high. Where such infrastructure is absent or dilapidated, as it is in many developing countries, sustained growth cannot take place.

Proper Incentives

Investments, however, are far from sufficient. They need to be guided by a sound set of economy-wide incentives. And proper incentives require macroeconomic stability and competitive markets. High fiscal deficits and high inflation prevent the proper functioning of markets and cause development to stumble. Where that is so, incentives can be put in order only by restoring and maintaining macroeconomic stability.

In addition, investments go to waste in an economy full of price distortions or blocked off from the rest of the world. Openness to global and domestic competition is essential for encouraging domestic producers to develop by adopting and adapting new products and techniques. Openness promotes the international flow of technology - through movements of people, foreign investments, imports, and exposure to foreign markets - and subjects domestic firms to the growth-stimulating rigors of international competition. When complemented by domestic competition, this exposure spurs innovation, the diffusion of technology, and the efficient use of resources. Conversely, systems of industrial licensing, restrictions on entering or exiting markets, and state controls on managers, employees and prices - all of which weaken the forces of competition - hold back development.

The Role of Institutions

Investments and policies are not made in a vacuum; they require well-developed institutions to give them shape and to make them effective. Well-functioning institutions are also critical for fostering competition, as the socialist economies in transition are finding out. Especially important is a legal and judicial system that secures property rights, safeguards contracts, and facilitates transactions. As important is a simple regulatory framework that is transparent and that does not stifle competition.

Heavy and misguided regulatory interference has hampered technological change and productivity growth in many countries, and has encouraged corruption and waste.

Countries need to provide the infrastructure for development while resisting interventions that are economically unproductive. An effective tax administration, to meet resource needs and equity objectives, and a strong central bank are key institutions that the state also needs to provide. Important too, is the capacity to conduct effective policy analysis and to implement policies well. And to take care of those who cannot care for themselves, safety nets to protect vulnerable groups need to be put in place. Where these institutions and institutional capabilities are absent - and they often are - they need to be developed (a time-consuming process that requires investments in the right type of human capital).

Interaction and Payoffs

It may not surprise anyone that each of these factors - investments, incentives, institutions - is important for development. But the evidence goes further, and some of it is more surprising. The history of development shows a strong synergism among investments, incentives, and institutions in development. Consider, for instance, the payoffs to combining investments and proper incentives. There are a number of examples of the disproportionate benefits of combining investments in people with ensuring competition. For instance, Eastern Europe did well in educational investment, but not in fostering competition. East Asia did well in both. And the difference in outcomes is striking.

Table 2.2 considers the interaction between economic policies on one side and investment in education and physical capital on the other. The combined impact of the two on GDP growth or on total factor productivity growth is especially strong. For instance, countries that invested in primary education or that fostered a competitive environment grew at about 3.8% during 1965-87. Countries that did both grew at 5.5%.

WHAT THE STATE MUST DO
FOR RAPID DEVELOPMENT

It may be unconventional today to focus on what the state must do rather than what the free market must do. But it really is not a question of state or market; each has an important and irreplaceable role. The dichotomy between intervention and laissez-faire is popular but false. It is more a question of a realignment of roles, of what the state must and must not do, and how, and what the market must be allowed to do, and how. In some areas, governments must take the lead, and in some, markets must be allowed to do so. The state is responsible for establishing a sound macroeconomic framework. The state also needs to ensure the provision of basic services, such as primary education and primary health care, and step in other areas where markets typically fail, such as infrastructure, poverty programs, and the environment.

Sound Macroeconomic Policy

For sustained progress, the state must put in place sound macroeconomic policies that keep fiscal deficits in check and exchange rates at realistic levels. Fiscal deficits result from rapid growth

Table 2.2

Interaction of Policy with Education and Investment, 1965-87

	Average GDP Growth	Average TFP Growth	Probability of higher than median GDP growth	Probability of higher than median TFP growth
Policy 'distortion' (a) and education (b)				
Low distortion and high education level	5.5	1.40	63.7	53.9
Low distortion and low education level	3.8	0.25	52.0	49.9*
High distortion and high education level	3.8	0.00	35.7	38.1
High distortion and low education level	3.1	-0.40	42.0	46.0*
Policy 'distortion' (a) and change in education (c)				
Low distortion and high rate of increase in education	5.3	1.30	57.0	54.3
Low distortion and low rate of increase in education	4.0	0.40	55.1	48.8*
High distortion and high rate of increase in education	3.5	-0.16	35.0	39.7
High distortion and low rate of increase in education	3.4	-0.19	39.2	44.7*
Policy 'distortion' (a) and investment (d)				
Low distortion and high investment	5.2	0.91	73.6	56.5
Low distortion and low investment	3.5	0.75	35.6	46.4*
High distortion and high investment	4.6	0.07	53.8	44.0
High distortion and low investment	2.6	-0.36	26.7	41.2*

Note: All results are significant at the 5 percent level unless marked with an asterisk (*), in which case they are not significant.

a) High distortion is reflected by a foreign exchange premium of more than 30 percent; low distortion, 30 percent;

b) Education is measured by the average years of schooling, excluding post-secondary schooling, of the population age 15 to 64. High education is defined here as more than 3.5 years; low education, 3.5 years or less.

c) Five-year increase (above or below the median).

d) Investment rate as a share of GDP (above or below the median).

Source: For foreign exchange premium, International Currency Analysis, Inc., various years. For all other variables, World Bank data.

in public spending or an insufficient tax effort. The losses of inefficient state enterprises are often a main contributor to excessive
spending - whether it occurs through direct budgetary transfers to
keep them afloat or through unrepaid loans from state-influenced
financial institutions. Therefore, reforms of the state enterprised
(such as liquidation of state marketing boards and privatization of
public enterprises) are often crucial to fiscal stability. Equally important is making the financial system commercially viable and de-linking
it from the government's "soft" budget.

When governments run large budget deficits, they absorb domestic saving and foreign funds, crowd out productive investments
by farmers, entrepreneurs, and larger businesses, and place the
financial system under great strain. Often too, large deficits induce
rapid inflation, which in turn exacerbates the deficit, creating a
vicious cycle. Deficits also lead to overvalued exchange rates that
stifle exports, damage domestic producers, and create pressures for
protection. Consider what happened in Indonesia and India in the
late 1980s. Indonesia had deficits of around 2.5 percent of GDP and
enjoyed stable, rapid growth. In India the deficit grew to nearly 10
percent of GDP, and the country bore the consequences in lost
competitiveness, reduced investment, and slower growth.

If large, persistent government budget deficits are the surest
route to economic failure, government policies that produce an
overvalued exchange rate will put a country on the same road almost
as quickly. Overvaluation leads inevitably to the rationing of foreign
exchange, which historically has meant that those in government
and their friends skim off large rents. Overvaluation creates pressure
for layer after layer of controls on imports, capital flows, and even
travel. And it destroys emerging export industries, perhaps the most
important foundation for growth for any developing country.

There is an easy and reliable way to identify unrealistic exchange rate policies: compare the official rate with the parallel
market rate. When the spread is wide, statistical studies demonstrate, growth slows, returns on investment decline, and the prospect
of financial crisis and capital flight increase. It is a myth that a strong
currency makes for a strong economy - the opposite is more nearly
the truth. The successful East Asian economies built their growth on
the export expansion created by depreciated real exchange rates.
China, whose manufactured exports now exceed India's by a factor
of more than 3, is a good example.

Critical Public Investments

How wisely a government invests in infrastructure and in people makes a critical difference for development. Governments that spread themselves too thinly neglect the tasks that only they can perform. The classic pattern is over-investment in new physical facilities and under-investment in repair and maintenance. Experience suggests that governments stay out of the production business, as many in East Asia have, provide more effectively for schooling and health care and create better infrastructure foundations for private business.

Small amounts of public investment in key sectors can make a huge difference. In many countries, government outlays in agriculture favour vast amounts of fertilizer subsidies, while small-scale irrigation schemes - often more than 80 percent cheaper than large ones - are neglected. So also are the basic tasks of agricultural research and extension.

Human investments are especially important. One of the greatest threats to the of low-income countries' future is the neglect of investments in basic health and primary education. The infant mortality rate in India is still nearly 100 per 1,000 live births, twice the rate in middle-income countries. Half the children in Pakistan do not enrol to primary school, compared to full enrolment in middle-income countries. But income is not the only reason social development lags; public policy makes a difference too. Sri Lanka and Guinea have the same income, but infant mortality is seven times as high in Guinea. Brazil and Uruguay have similar incomes, but people live seven years longer on average in Uruguay.

WHAT THE MARKET MUST BE ALLOWED TO DO

In practice, most governments have not performed adequately in the above-mentioned areas, where they have a legitimate role to play. Instead, they have been involved in a host of other spheres where the market would have played the lead role. In the process, they spread themselves too thinly, as a result, performed inefficiently, and also prevented the private sector from becoming the engine of growth. Governments need to do less in areas where markets work, or can be made to work, reasonably well. That means many countries need to deregulate and liberalize markets, and privatize many of the state-owned enterprises.

Domestic and External Liberalization

A permissive rather than a restrictive environment is essential for the private sector to flourish. The great debate over economic systems is over. Almost everyone agrees that communism is the longest way from capitalism to capitalism. For all their faults, competitive markets are the best way people have yet found to get goods and services produced and distributed efficiently.

What does creating a permissive environment for the private sector mean? For one, it means avoiding government monopsonies or punitive regulations. Examples of costly restrictions at various times include Argentina's policy of favouring incumbent firms for new industrial investment, and barriers to entry and exit in Brazil, China, India, Kenya, Zimbabwe or the previously socialist economies. The benefit of deregulation is evident from world wide experience. One example is the tremendous success attending actions of many African governments in abolishing agricultural marketing boards and moving towards a realistic exchange rate. Output of a number of key export crops, including cocoa, cotton and rubber, has increased dramatically since low points reached in the mid-1980s in countries such as Ghana, Nigeria, and Tanzania.

A permissive environment also means that market forces work freely to set prices, without price controls or large subsidies. Examples of failed price controls are numerous. Industrial performance lagged in industries subjected to such controls in Brazil, Egypt, Indonesia, and many other countries. Fertilizer policies in Bangladesh or India also show something else that is wrong with controls: some fortunate and well-connected farmers get all the fertilizer they want at low prices while less well-connected farmers find fertilizer much less available and more expensive.

More generally, a permissive environment is one in which the government seeks to reduce rather than increase the cost of doing business. That means reducing tariffs and quotas on international trade and integrating with the global economy. Successful countries have promoted openness to trade, investment and ideas as a means to encouraging domestic producers to cut costs by introducing new technologies and to develop new and better products. High levels of protection for domestic industry, conversely, has held development back by decades in many places. The effect of import competition on firms, for instance, in Chile and Mexico, and the effect of greater competition in export markets on firms in Japan and Korea confirm the decisive contribution to efficiency that the external economy can make.

Production and Distribution

It should not be the business of government to directly manage the production and distribution of private goods and services. Around the world, the record of public enterprise management is dismal. While it may be true in theory that a properly managed public enterprise can be as productive and efficient as a private one, the reality is that politics almost always intrudes and efficiency is the first casualty. Public enterprise managers are rarely permitted to shed excess labour to produce at minimum costs. And procurement is often treated as a way of enriching contractors and procurement officers rather than of producing efficiently.

Nigeria provides almost a textbook example of what can go wrong when the government gets directly into the business of producing goods and services. Between 1973 and 1990, the Nigerian public sector invested $115 billion, or just about $1,000 for every citizen. Yet there is no growth to show for this investment, and most public sector assets are operating at less than 40 percent capacity. The reason is that most of the investment was exorbitantly overpriced for what one might euphemistically call non-commercial reasons. Relying on the private sector to undertake major investments could have saved Nigeria up to $80 billion over the last 18 years since the oil boom.

Many countries, including Argentina, Ghana, Nigeria and Turkey, have initiated programs of privatization and reform of state-owned enterprises. Privatization has meant transferring assets to the private sector. Reforms of SOE's have included curtailment of their privileged access to the budget or credit system as well as trade and regulatory protection. Experience has shown that privatization is highly desirable as a means to achieving economic efficiency, but that it can be a difficult and slow process. Privatization needs to be combined with a variety of market reforms, such as price liberalization and deregulation - and the time-consuming process of private sector development and institution building.

TOUGH CHOICES FOR DEVELOPMENT

There is greater agreement today than at any time in recent memory, on the blend of actions, by the state and by the market, needed for successful development. This convergence of views, however, does not mean that all disagreements are over, or that the reform path to better performance is straightforward. For instance, there is still considerable debate about the role of the state in providing incentives for more rapid industrialization. In other areas, where the lead role of the state is clear, serious questions remain on how to improve the state's performance. And in areas where the state should clearly intervene less, political problems often constrain the state's ability to pull itself out the marketplace.

Let us look more closely at the issue of industrialization and the role of the state and consider whether the view presented in this paper conforms to the remarkable success of East Asian economies. In other words, did the governments of these economies go further in protecting industries and subsidizing credits to promote industrialization than the bounds for government actions identified here? The answer is yes. And would the economies have done as well without interventions? We do not know for sure, but the answer is probably no. And if that is the case, does it undercut the earlier conclusion on the limits of state intervention?

Not really. To show that, three features of the East Asian intervention deserve mention. First, the intervention was subjected to the market test of international competition. For example, export success was a key criterion for the provision of special incentives. Second, the intervention was flexible enough to be removed when it proved to be counterproductive. And third, the intervention was moderate to avoid undercutting price signals. So how replaceable is this type of intervention? Where it was put into effect as described above, the results were solid. But most countries were not able to follow these principles, and for them the interventions resulted in disaster.

But what about state activities in other areas? Does the state possess the capacity to effectively carry out the lead roles identified in the earlier sections? In many cases, people with the needed skills are available in the public sector, but they are misused. Redeploying staff from micro-managing wasteful industrial licensing schemes to implementing a child-feeding program for the urban poor is likely to have high payoffs. Moving the general manager of an obsolete state steel plant (which ought to be closed) to oversee a comprehensive road rehabilitation program will also yield benefits. Of course, public enterprises needs to be streamlined not only to redeploy labour, but also to foster development of the private sector, to reduce the waste in physical inputs and capital equipment, and to restore fiscal stability.

Finally, does the state have the sociopolitical will to reform its role for development? The state's sphere of effectiveness is clearly not limited to economic interventions. Political and social considerations determine what states do and these have a two-way relation with economic policy. On one side, social and political factors can limit economic progress. On the other, the right economic moves can reverse some of the sociopolitical factors constraining development.

Among the sociopolitical obstacles to development, corruption may be the most insidious, since it corrodes reforms for development, often forming a vicious cycle with political weaknesses and the resulting government interventions. Military expenditures can be another constraint, since they limit what can be spent on priority areas. Typically, under a fiscal austerity program, governments cut social expenditure while sparing military spending. Income inequality stemming from deep-seated social disparities also limit prospects for reform because of the large impact reforms can have on winners and losers. Often, regional and ethnic disparities undercut the very cohesion of a country.

All these problems can paralyse a government and make progress very difficult. But often, bold economic reforms go a long way toward correcting the basic imbalances and overcoming the political constraints. Together with redistributive and poverty-reduction programs, economic reform offers the best hope for achieving rapid development.

THE CHICKEN & EGG SYNDROME: DEVELOPMENT THEORY & DEVELOPMENT PRACTICE

Barry Lesser

The World Development Report 1991 is a review, *inter alia,* of development thinking/theory over the past four decades. Noting that, "Thinking on development has shifted repeatedly during the past forty years" (p. 4), the Report examines the changes which have taken place and presents what it feels to be the final "revealed truth" that has emerged from forty years of development experience. In all of this, one of the important questions to ask is why development thinking has changed as it has and, more importantly, whether we can now be confident that the truth has indeed been revealed and if so, what that truth is.

The Bank View

The Report itself suggests that we have moved away from certain theories because they have demonstrably failed to work over time in the sense that the countries which have ostensibly implemented or followed these theories have failed to achieve the expected results. If true, this may be a valid reason for change. But, as a basis for change, it is a proposition which begs three important questions:

a)   Why did we try these theories in the first place?

b)   Are the new theories any better in the sense that they derive from a stronger empirical base than the old ones?

c)   Is the apparent failure of the theories in fact a failure of theory or is it due to factors exogenous to the theory?

The Report suggests that in fact we now "know" many things which we did not know before. In particular it suggests that we now know that:

*   openness and competition are key elements to development success;

*   technological progress is the principal explanation for productivity differences between countries and that productivity differences are the key to explaining differences in growth of output between countries;

*   government intervention in the economy will help if it is "market-friendly" and hurt if not; and this means that governments should stay out of those areas where markets work reasonably well;

*   sound macroeconomic policy is essential to long term sustainable growth;

*   price distortions are a prime explanation for low growth performance;

*   individual freedoms are not inconsistent with economic growth;

*   people investments (education, health, etc.) are key to development success;

*   overall, government and markets are complementary; used properly each will contribute to achieving the maximum rate of growth and development.

This is an interesting list of things we are supposed to know. These are not the only things the report suggests we know but they are sufficient for present purposes to explore the questions raised earlier.

Part of what makes this list of "things we know" interesting, is that many of these "truths" are things which for many years economists and other social scientists have questioned, based in part on empirical observation. The technology argument, for example, would appear at least on the surface to discard the whole debate on appropriate technology and labour-intensive versus capital-intensive production processes. Thus, what represents "truth" may be more apparent to some than to others.

The Methodology of Economics

In economics, the test of any theory must be whether it yields results which accord with reality when tested against experience. If there is an existing body of experience which can be used for testing purposes, this paradigm works fine - a theory is formulated, tested and accepted or rejected depending on whether the tests confirm its conclusions/predictions. In the purest of views of this deductive methodology of economics, only the reality of conclusions matter; the reality of assumptions do not matter. In a less pure view, the reality of assumptions may be considered but the reality of conclusions remains paramount, i.e., a theory which is based on true assumptions but yields, for whatever reason, false conclusions, can never be accepted but one which uses false assumptions but yields correct conclusions, may be accepted even in the less than perfectly pure view.

In this deductive paradigm, theories may originate independent of experience but must ultimately be tested by experience. An inductive paradigm, by contrast, always takes experience as a starting point; theories are developed out of an examination of this experience. Which has been true of development thinking or theory over the last forty years or so? Has theory led experience or has experience led theory?

WDR 1991 suggests that theory led experience originally but now, with several decades of experience in hand, it is experience which is leading the theory. This is what, finally, has pointed us down the correct path. The old theories were tested by experience and found wanting while the new theories have been shaped by experience. Or so the Bank would have us believe.

One must realize that this does not mean that the standard deductive methodology of the economist has been supplanted. Rather it means that experience has shaped new theories which, in the opinion of the Bank, have been confirmed when tested in the usual way.

A Critical View of the Bank Position

What is the relevance of this discussion of economic methodology? There are, in fact, several points which emerge from this discussion which are germane to an evaluation of the paradigm of development theory espoused in WDR 1991. Consider:

1.   It is not correct to say that the old theories were not born out of experience. They were - the experience of the developed countries as of the end of WWII. The old theories were not developed in a vacuum. Their failure, if we agree they have failed, is partly a function of the fact that the development experience of European and North American countries proved not to be transferable without adjustment to the countries of Asia, Africa and Latin America. If this is true, then is there an equal possibility that the experience of the successes of the last twenty years, particularly the Asian NICs, on which much of the Bank's new theory rests, may prove to be not transferable to other developing countries? Is the validity of the assumptions behind the theory being overlooked?

2.   The old theories are said to have failed based on experience but were they in fact ever implemented under the conditions assumed by the theories? This is partly a question of whether assumptions do matter and partly a question of whether the *ceteris paribus* assumption of all these theories has been true. Certainly, governments have been far less benign forces than the old development theory would have them be and, equally, they have been subject to a host of external influences which, unambiguously, have affected domestic economic policy and performance.

3.   The Bank argues that experience shows the new theory to be true. It can be asked, however, whether all that has really been shown is that the old theories are false. If this is the case, then how do we know that this time we have it right? There are many who would argue that we don't know because we haven't proven the new theory to be true. They would argue, for one thing, that the evidence is not yet conclusive, even if it is suggestive, and that even if conclusive for the countries involved, there is little or no evidence to support the wholesale generalization of the same policy regime for every country.

4.   There is also a question which may be asked as to whether the new theory is in fact a "theory" or simply a collection of thoughts which, however, lack the internal consistency of a proper theory. If this is the case, does it matter? The answer to this is yes if it is to be used as a basis for generalizing to others, which is what the Bank has clearly been doing.

5.   The deductive methodology of economics means that economic theory is based on generalizations; it proceeds from the general to the particular. In this sense, it describes the average condition. Given this, the theory may never describe any particular situation at all. Averages are made up of some observations that are above average and some that are below average; it is only by coincidence that there any observations which exactly match the average. WDR 1991, however, tries to treat all countries the same and to prescribe the same general policies for all. There is a sense in which it is assuming that everyone, in practice, is the same as the average.

6.   One of the key assumptions of the empirical work on which the Bank analysis rests is that the international trade and financial system that is in place will remain in place. While the need to review the system may be acknowledged at times, the basic analysis takes the international order as given. In this context, the Bank "shows" that certain policies are most efficient. If the assumptions changed re the external environment, however, some of these conclusions might/would also change. The question then is whether the assumptions are justified. In different language, is the Bank using partial equilibrium analysis where general equilibrium analysis is required?

Or to put it differently still, is this a key assumption which does matter and which the failure to explicitly explore creates the artificial conclusion that the burden of adjustment rests exclusively with the developing countries? There is a clear basis for answering this question with a yes.

7.   Following on from the above discussion of averages, there is potentially a kind of fallacy of composition in the Bank model in the sense that what works for one country or a few countries will not necessarily work for everyone. For example, the prescription on trade regimes means, in practice, for many developing countries, export promotion. In turn, at least in the short run, this means increasing commodity exports. One country may well benefit from increasing its production and exports of, say, coffee or cocoa. But, if every producer of these commodities does the same thing, the price gets driven down, and the potential gains from the enhanced production are eliminated. This is at least a possible scenario. A counter-intuitive result is obtained because of the homogeneity assumption made by the Bank that everyone is the same.

8.   The Bank paradigm is one which favours market led development over state intervention but which also argues that poverty reduction and environmental integrity are equally important, along with growth, as elements of the development equation; there is an assumption/presumption that these three goals are complementary and yet there is no evidence offered to support this view nor is there any attempt to assess the record of the high growth, market-led economies in terms of either poverty reduction or environment.

These considerations are neither definitive nor exhaustive; they are simply illustrative of an argument that is meant to highlight four principal concerns regarding the Bank's views on development theory as expressed in WDR 1991:

a)   the evidence that we have finally discovered the "true" development paradigm is far from conclusive and the conclusion itself, if not wrong, is certainly premature;

b)   the implication of this paradigm that the same policies should apply to all, i.e., that the "truth" in terms of development is universal, ignores what is unique about individual countries and societies and runs the serious risk of over-generalizing to the detriment of all players; it is moreover a conclusion without particular quantitative support; no one has yet proven that what is true for one is true for all, and there is good reason to believe that it is not in this case;

c)   the assumption that the existing international order is a given may be correct but the failure to make it explicit disguises the fact that the domestic policy options explored may well be second best and generates no support, moral or otherwise, for industrialized nations to shoulder a greater share of the burden of adjustment;

d)   the presumption that market led growth will also give us environmental integrity and poverty reduction (not to mention gender equality and improved human rights) ignores some potentially very important trade-offs between these elements of development; the Bank's terminology of "market friendly" is meant to imply something short of total reliance on market forces but there is, nonetheless, an assumption that these goals can all be married without conflict in what the Bank paradigm clearly envisages as a market dominated system.

Conclusion

The thrust of these comments has been to examine some of the conceptual underpinnings of the development paradigm presented by WDR 1991 and the Report's own discussion of past development thinking. The paradigm itself has not been examined in detail although a number of individual aspects of the argument have been commented on. Rather the bulk of the discussion has centred on the question of whether the Bank has proven its case that, on the one hand, old development thinking, which emphasized the role of the state, has been largely discredited and, on the other hand, new development thinking , which emphasizes the virtues of market-led development, has been proven superior. What is suggested by way of an answer to these questions here is that no generalizations are possible (the failure to recognize this being one of the weaknesses of the Bank's own position) and there is clearly room to question the Bank's position at least for selected countries.

Unquestionably, there is room to question the proposition that the same policy prescriptions should apply to all countries.

For the Bank, the theoretical underpinnings for the policy regime it has already implemented or at least recommended in most developing countries under the label of structural adjustment are a matter of some importance. If you cannot sell the paradigm which lies behind structural adjustment as one which is theoretically defensible, you obviously have a problem in selling the policy of structural adjustment itself. Thus, it is no trivial exercise from the Bank's perspective to engage in the kind of review of development theory that is found in WDR 1991 nor, from this perspective, are the results surprising.

There can be no argument with the basic proposition that developing countries have failed to make the progress that thirty or more years of development efforts should reasonably have been expected to produce. Nor can there be any argument with the proposition that things cannot go on as they have been; something must change. But beyond this point, there is considerable room to debate what must change and for what purpose.

The Bank view is one which sees economic development and growth essentially as a generic process. What spells success for one spells success for all. But there is a sense in which this is precisely the view embodied in the very first development theories of the fifties and sixties, which used the historical experience of the developed countries as the basis for the theories of development expounded for the third world. More significantly, this universal prescription offered by the Bank ignores or discounts social and cultural characteristics of countries which do make a difference to the policies they adopt.

There is, in a sense, a World Bank/IMF hegemony which has been established out of the structural adjustment era of the 1980s and 1990s. What the Bank says and does, therefore, is of utmost importance to the policies and practices adopted by not only developing countries themselves but also developed country governments and bilateral ODA agencies in their dealings with developing countries. Thus, when the Bank claims that market-led development has been "proven" superior and that a new and "true" development paradigm has been found at last, this is an argument that must be treated seriously. More importantly, it is an argument that must be challenged, not because it contains no truth, but because it does not contain all truth.

Part of the challenge of development is not to force everyone into the same mold, with the same objectives and policies, but to search out common values where they exist and, otherwise, to learn tolerance and respect for the remaining differences. Development is very much a value-laden concept. So too is the Bank paradigm, which, *inter alia*, accepts the value system implicit in a market based economy and accepts growth as the paramount objective of development.

The world economy is showing an increasing trend towards globalization of markets, both product markets and production markets. With this globalization, we are also seeing pressures for harmonization of policies between countries as capital mobility and job (not labour) mobility make many industries, especially service industries, increasingly footloose, i.e., capable of moving quickly, cheaply and without loss of efficiency to any of several locations, which may be separated by large distances. But while this trend is very evident amongst developed, industrialized countries, it has not developed naturally or on its own amongst developing countries. The Bank paradigm would produce (impose) this result for the developing world. It is a paradigm which not only treats all developing countries the same as each other but also treats them the same as developed economies.

This is questionable partly because the assumption of homogeneity is questionable and partly because the policy regime involved in the Bank paradigm is only partly the same as the policy regime emerging in developed countries. One way in which the two differ is that there is no provision made in the Bank paradigm for changing the policy stance of developed countries *vis-a-vis* developing countries but there is provision for the reverse. In other words, the Bank paradigm, although ostensibly prescribing a common policy regime for all countries regardless of development status, is, in fact, asymmetric in this very important respect. This returns us to the argument made earlier about the failure of WDR 1991 to explicitly consider changes to the international order instead of, or in addition to, domestic policy changes.

The review of development thinking in WDR 1991 and the presentation of the "market-friendly" paradigm have much to commend them. But they suffer from a combination of not making their value judgements explicit, not making their assumptions explicit or making assumptions which may not be warranted, and generating conclusions which are not yet unambiguously proven on average and certainly not unambiguously established as best for any particular situation/country. The ultimate failure of WDR 1991, in this sense, is that it tries to do too much, to argue that there is a universal "development truth". If there is, it has not yet been discovered; certainly it is not in WDR 1991.

INTERNATIONAL AGENCIES AND NATION STATES: DIALOGUE FOR DEVELOPMENT?

Paul Bowles

The theme that I wish to address in this paper is the role that international agencies play in the interaction between the countries of the North and those of the South and whether this role can be said to be promoting the development of the South. In undertaking this analysis, my aim will be to demonstrate that the process of North-South interaction has changed significantly over the past 30 years and that underlying this change in process is a change in the assumptions about what it means to be a developing country. My conclusion will be that the present role played by international institutions does not promote the development of the South. A major reason for this is that the current dominant view of what it means to be a developing country is, in fact, theoretically and empirically false. The World Development Report 1991, by subscribing and indeed promoting this view, has therefore mis-specified the real challenge of development and the role that international institutions can play in meeting it.

In order to accomplish my task, I wish to focus on two key words in my title, namely, "dialogue" and "development". Let me start first with dialogue and analyze how the process of North-South interaction has changed. A brief historical note is useful here because it enables us to focus on change. Furthermore, a historical approach also enables us to see that underlying the changing nature of North-South dialogue are crucial assumptions about the structure of the international economy and, hence, our understanding of development.

During the 1960s and 1970s, the newly emergent post-colonial states of the South met as a group to negotiate with the countries of the North under the auspices of UNCTAD - the United Nations Conference on Trade and Development. It is true that this acronym also became known by some wags as Under No Circumstances Take a Decision, but, whatever the verdict on the importance of the results of this process, it was premised on the need for a forum for North-South negotiation. Under the auspices of UNCTAD, such issues as a code of conduct for multinational corporations, the volume of aid flows and the basis for a New International Economic Order were raised. The rationale for considering these issues was that international economic relations were seen as favouring the countries of the North. This bias resulted from, among other things, the North's monopoly of advanced technology, the oligopoly power of its corporations which dominate world trade and the declining terms of trade which acted to the disadvantage of the primary commodity exporting South. Under these circumstances, the market mechanism, left to itself, would not distribute the fruits of growth evenly. The role of international institutions such as UNCTAD, therefore, was to constrain market forces, mediate North-South disputes, and rectify unjust outcomes.

The purpose of this brief historical sketch is not to hark back to some "Golden Age" of development or to claim that international institutions met with much success in their endeavours. Rather, what is worth remembering is the nature of the process of North-South interaction and the underlying view of the international economy which laid the basis for such a process.

The process sketched above provides a sharp contrast with the structure of North-South relations today. Now the most important forum for the discussion of trade issues is the GATT - a forum in which developing countries have little say and where the main decisions and bargains are made by the U.S., the Europeans and Japan. The World Bank, furthermore, has moved to centre stage as being the international agency having the greatest impact on developing countries. In fact, the Bank along with the IMF, has become *the* major channel through which North-South economic interactions take place; UNCTAD is moribund and searching for a new role while the United States Nations Centre on Transnational Corporations has been abolished.

It is important to note, however, that not only have the players changed but so has the process. The South is no longer represented as a group, but the Bank and the IMF deal with developing countries on a case by case basis.

Why has this change of process come about? There are a number of possible explanations here. One is that the development experience of the past 30 years has varied greatly from country to country with some countries, notably in East Asia, doing very well whilst others, for example, those in sub-Saharan Africa, have performed poorly. The result of this has been that the coherence of the term the "South" has been lost and there is no longer a set of common interests which these countries share. Or perhaps it is that multinational corporations have not proved to be the ogres that they were once thought to be and that the rise of developing country manufactured exports has made the terms of trade debate less relevant.

There is some truth in these explanations although multinationals are even more dominant in world trade and investment and the bulk of developing country manufacturing exports come from a handful of countries. There are also some other important factors at play. Here we might think of the debt crisis which has forced many countries to abandon long term visions of changing the structure of the world economy and concentrate on acquiring short term financial assistance. The South with debts to the North of some US$ 20 trillion and annual net outflows to the North of US$ 50 billion is in no position to challenge the existing order. We might also refer to the end of the Cold War during the 1980s which robbed the South of one of its major bargaining chips, namely, the threat of defection to the socialist camp. With this threat gone, the North no longer has to address the concerns of the South as a group.

The change in players and the movement of the World Bank and the IMF to centre stage also deserves comment. In the 1980s there was a decisive shift in power towards capital in the countries of the North, as well as a rapid globalisation of capital. Agencies which preach liberalisation, the opening up of markets and the free movement of capital are likely to be the beneficiaries of these trends. Living as we do in an era of unprecedented bourgeois hegemony, it is easy to forget that the world has not also been this way and will not remain unchanged in the future.

It is perhaps surprising that the World Bank is so powerful, in view of the fact that net resource transfers have been relatively low during the 1980s and that by the end of the decade the Bank was actually receiving more in financial inflows from developing countries than it lent to them. Far from being a development *lending* agency, the Bank was taking in more money from developing countries than it was lending out; a situation which might be expected to reduce its importance to borrowing countries. However, the World Bank is no ordinary bank; its shareholders are the major industrial countries and its largest contributor the United States. This means that its power is not proxied by the profits which it makes but by the international context within which it operates.

In the 1960s and 1970s, the countries of the North and South met in forums such as UNCTAD to "negotiate". Now individual countries meet with the Bank and the IMF to undertake "policy dialogue". Dialogue presupposes a basic equality between the two participants; if one is in a much stronger position than the other then it is not so much dialogue as instructions. The changes in the international environment in the 1980s, to which I have referred above, suggest, I think, that the prospects for a genuine dialogue are slim. This does not, of course, mean that whatever the Bank says, or even whatever developing countries agree to do as part of structural adjustment programmes, for example, will necessarily be implemented. It is nevertheless clear who has the power in the relationship.

The changed process of North-South relations mirrors a change in the identification of what problems developing countries face. The World Bank deals with countries on an individual basis on the grounds that the international environment is given and that the major focus should be on internal reforms in order to position the country advantageously within this international economy; all developing countries are faced by the same external circumstances but some still do better than others. Therefore, the argument runs, the different outcomes must be the result of different internal policies. So, turning to the second key word of my title, does the new agenda encourage development?

A number of issues immediately suggest themselves. First is the question of what we mean by "development". This is, of course, an old question, but one worth asking often and one which has received fresh relevance in the light of the different emphases given in the World Bank's World Development Report with its emphasis on economic indicators and the UN's Human Development Report which places more emphasis on social indicators.

A second issue concerns the whole experience of structural adjustment programmes. Structural adjustment loans account for around 25 percent of total World Bank lending and there is now a substantial literature which has been critical of structural adjustment programmes (see, for example, the work of another international institution, UNICEF, presented in Cornia, Jolly and Stewart (eds.) *Adjustment with a Human Face*). Some critics have focused on the effects of the programmes on so-called vulnerable groups such as women and children, whilst others have pointed to the environmental consequences of encouraging cash crop production and agro-forestry exports.

These issues, the meaning of development and the efficacy of structural adjustment programmes, are important topics but here I want to raise a few other points. Before doing so, however, let me make clear that the case that I am going to argue does not mean that internal reforms in developing countries are not necessary. Many developing countries are characterised by great inequalities in access to resources and to political power; my point is not that developing countries are beyond criticism. Rather, my point is that the case for liberalisation is a mistaken panacea.

The 1991 Development Report is premised on the need for developing countries to adopt "market friendly" policies. Markets, it is argued, should be left to achieve a (static) efficient allocation of resources and this, combined with government provision of education, infrastructure and legal system, will promote dynamic efficiency (i.e. growth). Thus, countries should produce according to their comparative advantage (even, apparently, if they have a comparative advantage in being host to polluting industries) and integrate into the international economy on these terms. This will not only allocate resources efficiently now (domestically and internationally), but the stimuli provided by international competition will ensure that investment resources are also allocated efficiently and that, therefore, future growth is maximised.

In assessing this view of development and its policy prescriptions, I will focus on two points: what does this term "market friendly" mean; and, is the free market approach to development theoretically and empirically valid?

The term "market friendly" represents, on a charitable reading, a wonderful sleight of hand or, on a more critical reading, a deliberate obfuscation designed to deceive. "Market friendly" appears to indicate a *direction* of change - towards the market allocation of resources. However, it also implicitly suggests the desirable *end state*. Since friendship is presumably a good thing, then the more friendly you are to the market presumably the better the outcome i.e. a free market allocation of resources is optimal. This is left implicit because, as the Bank recognises, those economies of East Asia which have done spectacularly well, at least in growth terms, in the past 25 years have done so by using government actively in the economic sphere (of which more below). But to have suggested that what was required was to emulate their "guided markets" or "governed markets" would have left the door open for a role for government in the productive sector and some countries might have got the wrong idea and thought that government intervention of some types was alright. Better, therefore, to imply the desirability of markets by a term like "market friendly", which can always be defended as a direction of change if pushed!

Furthermore, even if one accepts the need to move in the direction of the market, the relationship between markets and ownership is not adequately explored. The implied position is that markets are only really compatible with private ownership; thus "market friendly" becomes "private ownership friendly". The Bank's view is that markets require both competition *and* private ownership to work effectively; the evidence for this proposition is scanty.

Nowhere is the deliberate obfuscation implied by the term market friendly more evident than in the Bank's attempt to lay claim to China's recent economic success. China has experienced rapid growth and doubled *per capita* output between 1978 and 1988; one of the shortest times in human history that such a record has been achieved. China has achieved such a record by moving away from a centrally planned economy and introducing market reforms. However, social ownership is still dominant with the state and collectively owned sectors producing more than 90 percent of total industrial output. Furthermore, significant state planning still exists, price controls are widely used, and there is no real "labour market". In short, China's success has been achieved in an economy in which market, planning and social ownership have all been in evidence. The Chinese economy is certainly very far from the free market economy which the Bank promotes and to suggest otherwise, by using the ambiguous term market friendly to describe the Chinese economy, is a deception.

A final point on market friendly. It is implied that it pays to be market friendly in all circumstances and no allowance is made for any second best outcomes. This is particularly relevant at present since the countries of the North became more protectionist in the 1980s. Given this, does it follow that it is always best for the countries of the South to liberalise their economies?

Let me move on to the view of development which the free market paradigm, as supported by the Bank, presents and assess the theoretical basis and empirical basis for this. The Bank's analysis implies that all countries are, for economic purposes, the same. A developing country is simply a poor country not one that has a structurally different relationship to the world economy than developed countries. Countries may differ in terms of resources endowments, income per head, etc., but there is nothing particularly different, from an economic point of view, about developing countries. They are subject to exactly the same economic laws as developed countries. Specifically, it implies that there is nothing exceptional in being, or attempting to become, a "late industrialiser"; there are no distinct policies which must be followed because development is taking place in the context of a world which is now characterized by large technological gaps, increasingly mobile international capital and a global competitive market. Developing countries are defined by their GNP per capita, rather than by their relationship to the world economy. This is a significant departure from the premises of the 1960s and 1970s.

Is it the case that developing countries are structurally similar to developed countries or do they face particular problems, which therefore require special policies, as a result of their position in the world economy? The free market paradigm, as we have seen, suggests that developing countries do not face theoretically distinct problems; the theory of "late industrialisation" suggests otherwise.

The theory of "late industrialisation" views the state's intervention in the development process as a crucial factor. This theory has a long history going back to debates about how Germany, Russia and the United States overcame the disadvantages of backwardness in the 19th century to compete with Britain; perhaps its most well known exponent being Gerschenkron. This theory has received further recent exposition from Amsden. For Amsden, the significant feature of those economies that have successfully industrialised in the Twentieth century is that they have done so by learning. In a world where over 95 percent of Research and Development takes place in developed countries, the ability of developing countries to compete on the basis of innovation is severely curtailed. However, competing on the basis of cheap labour alone is also problematic and unlikely to lead to sustained growth; what is needed therefore is the ability of developing country industry to learn. This contrasts with the first industrial nation, Britain, which gained preeminence through invention and the Nineteenth century industrialisers who did so on the basis of innovation. Amsden argues, therefore, that the large technological gap which exists between rich and poor countries in the Twentieth century can only be closed if the poor countries create the institutions enabling them to learn. The state, always an important actor in the growth process, is a central institution for late industrialisers. Amsden writes:

To catch up in the twentieth century has required still heavier doses of government support because backwardness has been relatively greater...Not only have states in late industrialising countries intervened by protecting infant industries. They have also intervened by providing private investors with a battery of incentives that, simplified, boil down to subsidies. The tariff epitomizes the age of infant industry protection. The subsidy, which includes tariff protection and financial incentives, epitomizes the struggle to industrialize after the Second World War...

...The state in late industrialisation has intervened to address the needs of both savers and investors, and of both exporters and importers, by creating multiple prices. Some interest rates are higher than others. Importers and exporters face different prices for foreign currency. Insofar as the state in late industrialization has intervened to establish multiple prices in the same market, the state cannot be said to have gotten relative prices "right", as dictated by supply and demand. In fact, the state in late industrialization has set relative prices deliberately 'wrong' in order to create profitable investment opportunities (Amsden 1989, pp. 13-14).

The conflicting demands placed upon the economic system of late industrialisers requires that an active state intervene to mitigate these conflicts. Instead of exposing the economy to the full force of international market forces, the state mediates and tempers these forces and protects and fosters its own learning industries. Identifying which industries and sectors to promote is a relatively manageable task for late industrialisers. As Wade writes with respect to Taiwan, "the fact that Taiwan has not been near any world technology frontier until very recently make the selection of 'winners' easier than for more advanced countries" (1990, p. 189). Far from 'getting prices right', a key element in the state's armoury to support such targeted industries has been the subsidy.

Thus, the state plays the crucial role of entrepreneur in late industrialisation, directs resources to target sectors and fosters industrial development through subsidies and shields the economy from the ravages of international market competition. The reason why state intervention was necessary is precisely because market forces, far from being friendly to developing countries, can be destructive; the market destroys not protects the weak and late industrialising countries have therefore had to temper the operation of market forces and to use them selectively.

Empirical support for this theory comes from two of the most successful "late industrialisers", namely, South Korea and Taiwan. These countries (and before them Japan) have achieved their economic success by directly intervening in the market, by tightly controlling the financial system, by directing credit to specific sectors, by using selective import controls and export promotion measures, and by having active industrial and technology policies. The remarkable economic performance of the two East Asian economies, therefore, does not owe its success to the application of free market principles and adherence to the static concept of comparative advantage; in many ways, they created their comparative advantage.

The Bank sometimes recognises that the success of Taiwan and South Korea did not result from the application of neoclassical economic principles, but still does not advocate interventionism elsewhere. Rather, the Bank tries to square the circle by arguing that although the East Asian countries were successful in using interventionist policies, other countries do not have the capacity or commitment to intervene to the same effect. For them, it is argued, the non-interventionist route is the most appropriate. This, however, is a *non sequitur*.

It is perfectly true that the East Asian "model" is not capable of being universally replicated but this is not simply a matter of insufficient "technical expertise". In part, the non-replicability arises because of the internal structure of the East Asian economies which enabled a relatively autonomous state to discipline capital in return for subsidies. The same state structures, and class compositions of the state, do not occur in many other developing countries.

However, another crucial difference is in the external conditions. The East Asian countries were uniquely positioned within the international economy because of their strategic significance in the Cold War. This gave them privileged access to U.S. financial resources and export markets at crucial points in their development. The American support at no point resembled a blank cheque but it is clear that these countries were favoured in their trading relations with the U.S. - a favour which they exploited to the full.

The account of the basis of the East Asian countries' success offered here means that the World Bank's position is robbed of its foundations on two counts. Firstly, these countries did not use the free market internally to promote their development. Secondly, external conditions played a critical part in determining their success. The fact that other developing countries do not face such favourable external circumstances means that for the East Asian model to be generalised a necessary condition is that the external environment itself must change.

It is here that an important role for international institutions exists and the challenge of development is to fashion the institutions and policies capable of giving all developing countries the same external chances that the East Asian countries had.

It should be the role of international institutions to constrain international market forces and carve out for developing countries the room to manoeuvre which they so manifestly require. The unleashing of market forces in the South will not favour those at the bottom of the international pecking order no matter how much those at the top stand to gain.

REFERENCES

Amsden, A. *Asia's Next Giant: South Korea and late Industrialization*. Oxford: Oxford University Press, 1989.

Wade, R. *Governing the Market: Economic Theory and the Role of Government in East Asian Industrialization*. Princeton: Princeton University Press, 1990.

DOES DEVELOPMENT
ASSISTANCE MATTER?

A.D. Tillett

The two most important features in aid over the last ten years - a period which has seen official development assistance increase from $37.8 bn in 1980 to $62.6 bn in current values - have been the abandonment of projects in favour of programs, and a conflict between aid for growth and aid for development. In both cases, because of its central position within the aid system, the IBRD has been in the forefront. This role has less to do with the total value of its disbursements than its predominant policy leadership. The Development Assistance Committee (DAC) reports that International Financial Institutions (IFIs), which include the World Bank Group, accounted for no more than 9 percent of total resource flows from developed to developing countries and they:

> ...in addition to being funding institutions, have important cata-
> lytic effects on other official and private sources and play a
> central role in policy advice as well as transfer of management
> skills in the largest sense.[1]

The Bank's concentration on comprehensive programs, consistent
with its findings in the *World Development Report*, increases this
influence, which, when taken together with donor fatigue - a combination of declining political support, uncertain results and trade
myopia - provide it with a preeminent place in defining the responses of industrial countries to development issues.

Background

Information and ideas about aid are coordinated through the
Development Assistance Committee of the OECD. Most official
development aid is provided by the industrial countries which constitute its membership.[2] The reduction of oil producers' surpluses
together with the demise of the Soviet Union have left developing
countries with few alternatives.[3] Non DAC countries net disbursements amounted to $9,969 mn (US $) in 1990 or 20 percent of
DAC's net disbursements. This total reversed a trend, principally
because of the Gulf War, and demonstrated that aid is provided as
much for political as developmental reasons. Official development
assistance is principally an issue involving the industrial market
economies - directly through bilateral aid or as subscribers to the
World Bank Group and supporters of the UN system - and the aid
recipients, the developing countries which are listed in Table 5.5.
DAC members are required to follow common rules, for example
distinguishing aid from trade concessions (which are loose enough),
and their common policy orientation which is increasingly responsive to policy ideas of their Finance Ministries and the World Bank.

Total Resource Flows

Development assistance is only one portion of the total resource flows from industrial to developing countries. Changes in the
composition of the total resource flows are important in order to
understand the increasing weight of foreign aid (or overseas development assistance) and to appreciate the difficulties facing recipients.
Total resource flows are divided into Official Development Finance
(composed of Official Development Assistance and other Official

Development Finance); export credits; and private flows, which have five components, including direct foreign investment and bank lending. It is the relationship between ODA and private flows which are the most important.

At first sight, total resource flows appear satisfactory, increasing from $128.3 bn (1980) to $144.2 bn (1990) in current dollars (US); but when calculated in 1989 dollars, the figures show a decline from $179.4 bn to $128.9 bn. Moreover, official development aid, when compared with private flows, is now more, not less, important to developing countries (see Table 5.1); and within ODA, multilateral disbursements declined in 1989. The choice of these two dates disguises rather than illuminates the changes during the decade, for between 1982 and 1989, disbursements fell below their 1980 figure of $128 bn reaching a trough of $81.8 bn in 1986.

Table 5.1

Total Resource Flows to Developing Countries
(current $bn)

	1980	1990	% 1980	1990
I Official Development Finance	45.6	78.8	35.5	54.6
(a) ODA	37.8	62.6	29.5	43.4
(b) ODF	7.8	16.2	6.1	11.2
II Total Export Credits	16.5	4.6	12.9	3.2
III Private Flows	66.2	60.8	51.6	42.2
(a) Direct Investment	11.2	32.0	8.7	22.2
(b) International Bank Lending	49.0	18.5	38.2	12.8
which is short term	26.0	-	20.3	-
(c) Total Bond Lending	1.6	0.8	1.2	0.6
(d) Other Private	2.0	5.0	1.6	3.5
(e) NGO Grants	2.4	4.5	1.9	-
Total Net Resource Flows (I+II+III)	128.3	144.2	100.0	100.0

Source: *Development Co-operation*, (1991), T. V1-1, p. 113.

The first discussion point is: *how can total resources for developing countries be increased?*

Total resource flows will either come from a growth in the proportion of ODA or direct foreign investment, the latter being the largest component of private resource flows. The Bank's calculations, using slightly different figures, show that net resource flows to developing countries are estimated to increase from US $63.3 bn (1989) to $103 bn in 1995, of which private flows grew the most rapidly from $26.7 bn to an estimated $47 bn; and direct foreign investment will form 75 percent in 1995.[4] The Bank is assuming renewed industrial country flows in all categories with an emphasis on the 'compensation principle' - the replacement of aid by private investment.

How realistic is this assessment? What does it mean when aid - even at today's admittedly inadequate levels - is compensated by direct foreign investment flows? The following Table compares direct foreign investment as a percentage of aid received in 1989 by listing the number of countries in which DFI is greater than aid, and therefore are currently fully compensated; countries which are 'probably compensated' (their current DFI is over 75 percent of official development assistance); and 'potentially compensated' (between 50-74 percent). Only 21 countries of the 100 low and middle income countries fall into the three categories.

Table 5.2

Aid and Direct Foreign Investment

Aid Level (US $ mn)	DFI 100 +	DFI 75 +	DFI 50 +
500 +	2	-	1
250 - 499	1	-	1
100 - 249	5	2	3
100 -	5	1	-
Total	$2,906 (13)	$320 (3)	$1,743 (5)

Although the exercise is static and based on the assumption that the lack of official development aid can be replaced without effecting growth, which is in itself an unlikely possibility, the Table forces us to recognize that the replacement - or even something near it - of ODA by DFI will be at best highly selective and at worst, punitive.[5] There are only two low income countries (Angola and Myanmar) in the above Table and both could well be abberations because of the chosen year. In sum, both aid and private flows must increase for developing countries to grow.

Programs for Growth

If we agree that resources should grow (total resource flows are about 24 percent of the developing country exports) and we assume that private and official flows are unlikely to increase, how should development assistance best be used?

The Report comments:

> Because of the impact of the debt crisis on private sector lending to the developed world, bilateral and multilateral grants and loans will most likely contribute more than half of all resource flows to developing countries in the 1990s. An adequate volume of these flows is therefore crucial. The quality of these flows could be raised through increased co-ordination among aid and finance agencies; more effective support for market oriented policy measures (providing greater support for fewer but more ambitious reforms); stronger emphasis on supporting private sector initiatives; greater attention to environmental policies; and features that "insure" debt creating flows against price and interest rate volatility (p. 150).

If total resource flows are insufficient then the Bank's pragmatism becomes more acceptable and aid should target developing countries to support their credit-worthiness with the aim of becoming attractive to investors. So, the most useful (and important) objective for ODA is to encourage other resource flows, particularly direct foreign investment; for this to occur, aid should concentrate on improving the investment climate and strongly support private sector activities.

A second question, closely related to the first, is: *should development assistance be used to encourage private resource flows as a long term solution for developing countries?*

There must be a concern in using aid, a scarce commodity, when there are other, and potentially easier, ways to increase resource flows. The first is the issue of trade barriers, and particularly agricultural trade barriers, which are analytically (although admittedly not practically) independent of the ability of developing countries to take advantage of markets. Unless industrial countries practice trade reform and the move to implicit or explicit trading blocs are removed, only a select few developing countries will be able to take advantage of renewed world growth.[6] Further, and with potentially greater short term impact, there is the continuing presence of the debt. The Report demonstrates the increasing damage of high interest payments to the developing countries' economic performance and its impact through transfers; not only are net transfers, when compared to resource flows, negative - an absurd situation by which developing countries have returned more than they have received[7] - but interest payments have had a counterproductive effect on trade performance. There were only 11 countries in 1989, out of 100 developing countries, with a positive balance of payments position (increasing to 14 if official transfers are included) and more than 41 countries had a debt service to export ratio over 20 percent; 22 had a ratio of over 30 percent. A reduction in debt service (principal and interest repayments on long term debt) by ten percent would equal aid flows (developing country exports amount to $516,460 mn compared to aid flows of about $48 mn) and presumably increase exports from industrial countries. External debt may be a "complex brew" but it surely contains the potion of growth.

Aid for Growth or Development?

If we equate market support programs as encouraging developing country growth (with the promise that increasing wealth is a condition of development) and investing in people (support for health, education and general living conditions) a key development function, then the *World Development Report* reflects an ambiguity which is not easily reconciled. Market friendly measures are increasingly the result of finance for policy measures (price incentives, exchange rate adjustments, and trade liberalization); measures which depend for their success on factors which neither the Bank nor the majority of countries have much control. Although program lending has been growing as a proportion of total aid and accounted for 13.3 percent of total bilateral and 5.7 percent of multilateral aid, it is not clear if these programs have been successful. The *WDR* admits that the indicators pointing to the success of adjustment programs are not "straightforward" and that, in particular, the social adjustment component shows "no clear relation between adjustment and changes in employment or social indicators."[8] Other Bank publications are more forthright noting that "about 60 percent of all conditions in structural adjustment loans and sectoral adjustment loans were implemented fully or more than fully" while admitting that there was "great variation" in implementation. Accepting that adjustment programs are difficult to judge or implement, it is interesting to note that the Bank's solution, or future directions,[9] emphasise prerequisites and ensuring that the key conditions are met before the loans are fully activated. In other words, adjustment loans will be provided when there is agreement about the causes and not simply the problem. It is important to recall that program lending is often a qualification for other Bank supported loans and bilateral support. Policy co-ordination may result in donor efficiency but it can lead to an unfortunate consensus which may be less the result of wisdom than a combination of self assurance and self protection.

The increasing support for program lending can be compared to education loans, which the Report regards, correctly, as a value in itself. In 1990, bilateral support for education amounted to 11.5 percent of bilateral agency disbursements and 4.6 percent of total disbursements of multilateral agencies in 1990. If education is so important, should it not be treated as valuable as loans and interest repayment? If health and other social programs are added to education, social expenditures amount to 22.8 and 17.8 percent for bilateral and multilateral disbursements, respectively. There is little consistency in earmarking this essential growth element.

The next question must be: *should investments in people be treated independently (perhaps autonomously) from short term growth or stabilization programs?*

The value of a donor consensus which protects social rights not only increases social equity but protects the weakest who most deserve support, especially in vulnerable economies that depend on aid to function or perhaps survive. Table 5.3 summarizes information found in Table 5.4 (p. 80); it discriminates countries by the value of aid flows to the total value of goods and services (the Gross Domestic Product) and then rank orders them by the degree of aid dependence. A similar calculation, using World Bank data, is presented for comparison as Table 5.5 (pp. 81-83).

Table 5.3

Aid Dependency, 1989

Aid Category	Countries	Aid Value (US $ mn)	Percent
Highly Dependent (20 +)	14	3,736	12
Dependent (10)	25	7,089	21
Influenced (5-9)	16	6,116	18
Other	95	16,950	49
Total	160	34,120	100

Source: see Table 5.4 (p. 80).

Highly aid dependent countries, for example, receive the equivalent of 20 percent plus of the value of their GDP; aid dependent, between 10 and 20; and aid influenced, between 5 and 9.9 percent of GDP. These countries urgently need aid to maintain their economies on which donor agencies, and the World Bank, have a major influence (not to say considerable power) over. If there is any set of countries where donor influence should prevail, it is the categories of highly and dependent aid recipients. Yet, donor sponsored social investments make up a very small percentage of their total aid flows. As Table 5.4 shows, only 12 of the 57 countries receive more than 20 percent of their social investment expenditures from donors.

Therefore: *should donor countries ensure that a fixed proportion of their funds is disbursed for social programs? Should we work for a reverse conditionality?*

In this case, donors would take a relatively aggressive stand; social commitments to recipients would be key for continued aid flows. Agreements would and could be reached less about economic management and more about social management. If aid dependency continues, and there is little optimism that world economic growth or policy reform can easily reduce the need of official development assistance to aid dependent countries, donors and recipients should act on the weight of evidence regarding social programs and negotiate around these development criteria rather than purely financial and policy matters. At a time when the trend is downward, there is a strong case, found in this report, for massive educational adjustment.[10] A discussion between donors and recipients regarding social programs, on the basis of social rights, is preferable and more straightforward than the current concern, again found in the Report, regarding the tricky issue of governance.

Effective policy making, the Bank argues, can only come with institutional restructuring and state reform; these changes, which require "political courage and economic vision" are expected to lead to better government and better decisions. Few can deny that institutional robbery - in both developed and industrial countries - in favour of the rich and powerful is a moral offense if the poor suffer. The Report assumes that the creation of a framework of opportunities by which agents can exercise their rational self interest is an adequate guardian of economic as well as political and social rights. Moreover, it proposes -and here it makes a further appeal to aid coordination - that institutional and policy reform rather than financial criteria alone become the new zone for donor conditionality. To quote:

> In countries that are not paralysed by political forces, and where reforms can go forward, the task for external aid and financial agencies is to promote it. They can do this by avoiding support for unproductive activities or for new products that would be implemented under severely distorted conditions. In many countries, external agencies must help to strengthen the public institutions without which development assistance is likely to be ineffectual.[11]

Thus, external aid agencies, given the number of aid dependent countries, become arbiters. The historical record is not a positive one because today's reforms often become tomorrow's errors - *pace* large dams; or consider the record of the donor agencies regarding environmental costs. Further, even if there is a verbal consensus regarding the present value of the environment principally to industrial countries - where most of the pollution originates - it is not clear that the same concern is shared by resource rich developing countries (e.g. Malaysia and Brazil). Moreover, there is a logical - not to say political - difficulty in making governance or institutional reform the new conditionality; can you order a country to be democratic?

Donor agencies should follow the logic of their research and provide funds for social development - and they should do it both indirectly and directly. Indirectly, by matching funds to recipient governments' social expenditures, and directly to educational institutions, by, for example, earmarking funds for NGOs in developing countries. If long term growth is based on human resource development, then policies should acknowledge that as people become more knowledgeable, they demand greater rights - a valuable if difficult by-product of global communication - so that educational expenditures, per family, increase as much as consumer goods as per capita income grows. CIDA's WID policy-direct support for women in development is surely a step in the right direction; the impact of women on the structure and opportunities for the family (the basic unit of any social infrastructure) is fundamental. The concern is that WID and other social development policies do not offer a quick enough return for politicians and bilateral aid bureaucrats, and so they and the institutions that they run may not stay on course.

Global Problems

The case for global official assistance is the reverse of the current practice of bilateral aid. As noted, bilateral aid often seeks leverage and political advantage with client countries and, in the process, redefines the spirit as well as the definition of overseas development assistance. For example, administrative expenses, military and police training as well as private sector market studies are all defined as part of a country's ODA budget; very soon the reconstruction and reform in Eastern Europe and the ex-Soviet states may be added to this small pot. Although the definition of aid urgently requires revision, the most disadvantageous aspect of bilateral aid is that its national ownership rarely permits it to grapple with global problems. Multinational institutions, such as the World Bank Group and the UN system, are being asked - a feature of the New International Order - to do more with less.

The preservation and improvement of the world environment is one of the most urgent and pressing challenges; we all agree that to dent these issues requires not only common goals but collective action. The UN Environment and Development Secretariat calculates that developing countries will need $125 bn per year into the foreseeable future to ensure environmentally sustainable growth. This figure does not include the costs of global clean-up in developed countries. Global development problems require secure and independent funds, and innovative ways of obtaining them.

Has the time come for a global tax system, levied on individuals and not governments? A world citizenship tax?

Given our biology and history, should we not accept that there are some common basic properties of the world and our heritage that we want to preserve, independent of our nationality? Further, that the United Nations system, for all its weaknesses, is the only current enterprise which has the potential for dealing with global issues, even though its current performance can be - and is - criticized. For the UN, or any alternative system, to work successfully, it should have its own resources; at present the UN does not levy taxes and depends on the largesse - and so agreement - of the larger nations.[12] The potential for the UN as a global system (which represents our common interests) is slowly being formed (with amoeba like speed) as a consensus grows that there are common properties (the heritage of humankind) which we should preserve for our children (whatever nationality, race, colour or creed). In the past, "who owned the moon?" was a school child's joke. With the commencement of space flight, seabed exploration, the reduction in air quality and Chernobyl, compounded with the knowledge that world population will grow to 8.5 bn people in 2025, the use of finite natural resources - the ownership of the global commons and therefore inter-generational rights - becomes even more urgent. The arguments for a global taxation system are skilfully examined in Ruben Mendez's *International Public Finance* which will soon become, in my view, an indispensable source for the development debate.[13] Given the urgent problems faced by the United Nations, taxpayers should be given the right to designate tax dollars for international agencies of choice - and receive a tax credit - as bilateral donor agencies make world environment and other agreed common interests priorities of official aid.

Popular Support?

The demand for aid grows. Its supply is diminishing as industrial countries increasingly look for discretionary funds to use in other, more pressing, domestic areas. One cannot but suspect a secret pleasure in advocating developing country economic reform together with the promotion of private flows; it removes responsibility from hard-pressed governments (without abandoning the joys of the moral high ground). To ordinary citizens, however, aid arguments must seem arcane because the issues are not simply technical - which instruments to use? - but rests on an underlying question - what is aid for?

Many citizens have straightforward answers. The Canadian Government, to take one example, undertakes public attitude surveys which record that Canadians regard food, health and shelter as the most important obstacles to be overcome by developing countries; that aid should relieve suffering and that churches and charitable organizations (followed by the United Nations) are the most effective partners; while, on the other hand, there are increasing doubts that aid sent to poor countries gets to the people who need it most. A growing number of Canadians believe, with well over one half strongly agreeing, that "Canada should help the needy in Canada first."[14]

The strong message, as it has been since the surveys began, is people first; this is because, most Canadian taxpayers - and one presumes taxpayers in other countries - like to see direct results. Elected governments have to pay some heed to public views if development aid is to be maintained as a relatively constant item of public expenditure, and so industrial country governments, such as Canada, take the people perspective into account.

Should governments, like that of Canada, follow a more popular, people-directed aid program (which would, given constant or declining aid flows, reduce bilateral leverage between industrial donors and developing country recipients)?

The arguments for an expansion of people to people programs are in the Report and one would have thought that such
arguments might be favoured by governments interested in reducing
the costs of the public service. First, non-governmental agencies, in
general, are less costly and their dollar delivery value more efficient;
second, their mandates emphasise personal experience and resolv-
ing human problems on a micro scale - the scale where most
development takes place; and third, a Canadian discussion point
perhaps, as our country becomes more multicultural, there is an
urgent need to understand different cultures *in situ*. The Peace
Corps was an important influence in attempting to reverse the
insularity of a generation in the United States. We, in Canada, are
beginning to have cultural myopia about how people should behave
and the rules they should follow; multiculturalism might become a
new puritanism relying on the idea of different experiences rather
than the experience of different cultures. Work and education in
different countries - in this case developing countries and through
NGOs - will have a salutary impact on Canada's future ability to deal
with multicultural social problems. If the idea seems familiar, it is it is
an endorsement for the old CUSO.[15]

There is, also, a need for greater knowledge about the work of
development agencies and their high probabilities of failure. Politicians - who increasingly speak for development agencies and see
them as goody bags to round off bouts of international tourism -
believe that a realistic discussion would be fatal to development aid.
Thus, the system works, from NGO to government official (and in
spite of the evidence) to demonstrate success. After thirty years of
projects and programs, one would hope for greater realism, openness and focus; one would hope for the didactic spirit of *The
Challenge of Development*. The World Bank, for example, pub-
lishes its evaluation results where one can read that 70 percent of
projects are considered satisfactory, but that the percentage of
satisfactory projects has been falling since operations evaluations
commenced in 1974.[16] There is no such series for the Canadian
International Development Agency (CIDA) and, one suspects, for
most bilateral agencies. The unwillingness to discuss aid performance (thirty percent is a good record when compared to industrial
projects and innovation launches here) is a deficiency of bilateral
agencies to act professionally and to treat citizens and their views

seriously. If current aid practice is poor, it should be abandoned, but it is no response to aid fatigue to announce yet another policy and expect, without evidence, taxpayers to trust government declarations alone. In future, there should be a much greater emphasis on publishing evaluations and discussing their results with citizens and stakeholders. It is possible, of course, that the results will turn taxpayers away from development aid, but the discussion will allow an examination of the how and why of our relations with developing countries, and our attitude as an industrial country which seems more and more, only to regard them as potential consumer markets. But aid and trade are different; the public survey results confirm this view.

Canadian Institutions

Canadian institutions, such as the Canadian International Development Agency and the International Development Research Centre, are undergoing change, driven, in part, by the current government's wish to reduce and simplify their administrative costs and, it seems, to respond more directly to the government's view of Canada's national interests. The Canadian aid program disbursed about $ 2.5 bn in 1990, approximately .5 percent of GDP and about 1.7 percent of the federal budget. In total aid disbursements it ranks about eighth among DAC members. There are many points which can and have been made about these changes, but they are in essence questions about Canadian experience and values.

Should Canada continue to have an aid program, and if so, what should be its objectives?

Canada has a notable development tradition and it should be used to answer this pressing issue - not as promoters but as professionals. The general disillusion with aid could end, and perhaps should, the current role of our development agencies. Is there a special place for Canadian expertise and its development tradition or should Canada become an exemplary world citizen and subordinate its national interests and program into a global or multilateral aid force? Can relatively small programs avoid demonstrating their national value (to business and other interest groups) and maintain the value and integrity of aid? Or should Canada use a combination of private companies and non-governmental agencies (trade and humanitarian aid) to deliver the aid program? The virtue of the *Challenge of Development* is that it raises these issues which require, if there is to be a renewed Canadian development program, answers.

NOTES

[1] *Development Co-operation, 1991*, p. 119.

[2] Australia, Austria, Belgium, Canada, Finland, France, Germany, Italy, Japan, Netherlands, New Zealand, Norway, Sweden, Switzerland, United Kingdom, and the United States.

[3] Non DAC Aid is provided by Spain, Portugal, Luxembourg and Iceland who are members of the OECD but not the DAC Committee, Central Europe and the Soviet Union, Arab countries (principally Kuwait and Saudi Arabia), and a number of developing country donors including, at different times, China, India, Venezuela, Korea and Taiwan. In 1980, their total disbursements amounted to $13 bn and in 1990 around $10 bn. principally from Arab countries.

[4] See T.1.3, p. 24. Although DFI is expected to grow more quickly than officials grants and loans, non DFI private flows are expected to grow even more rapidly suggesting that bank loans will resume to developing countries. DFI constituted 84 percent of private flows in 1989.

[5] The *WDR* notes that "they will *probably* remain concentrated in globally integrated, middle income countries with well developed infrastructure"(p. 24, emphasis added).

[6] "Between 1966 and 1986, the share of imports affected by all non tariff measures increased by more than 20 percent for the United States, almost 40 percent for Japan and 160 for the EC" (p. 104).

[7] See Fig. 6.5, p. 126. Aggregate net resource flows are net flows on the long term debt, plus grants and net foreign direct investment. Transfers are aggregate net resources minus interest payments on long term loans and repatriation of profits.

[8] The Report puts this down to a lack of data (p. 115).

[9] See *World Bank Annual Report, 1989*, p. 78-81, for this discussion. The future directions also include limiting Bank adjustment loans in order to protect projects and sectoral support and [10] See Box 3.6, p. 68, where bilateral and multilateral aid is recorded from 1980-88.

[10] See Box 3.6, p. 68, where bilateral and multilateral aid is recorded from 1980-88.

[11] See p. 147 which continues to advocate attention to social adjustment programs. In a previous passage, the Report acknowledges the difficult choices facing donor agencies under extreme economic conditions.

[12] The United States, for example, deliberately pays its quotas three months late in order to emphasise - as if an institution in New York needed such a reminder - that it is the greatest financial contributor to the system.

[13] Now published by the Oxford University Press, 1992. The book reviews most of the arguments found here from the valuable perspective of international public finance.

[14] Published by CIDA, different years since 1986.

[15] See Ian Smillie, *The Land of Lost Content: A History of CUSO* (Toronto, 1985).

[16] See Annex 1, *Evaluations Results for 1989*, p. 93. The series discusses why some projects succeed and others fail.

Table 5.4

Aid Dependency: GDP & Social Investment, 1989

Country	ODA (mn $)	% GDP	% Social Investment
Highly Aid Dependent			
Gambia	94	52.2	15.9
Mozambique	759	49.0	7.8
Somalia	440	45.4	11.6
Solomon Is.	48	36.9	-
Maldives	28	35.0	25.9
Vanuatu	39	32.5	2.6
Eq. Guinea	42	30.0	0.0
Malawi	394	29.8	5.4
Chad	329	28.1	10.6
Samoa	27	27.0	6.5
Mali	470	26.1	13.8
Tanzania	918	24.3	8.5
Mauritania	195	21.4	13.0
Comoros	43	21.5	2.0
Subtotal	**3,736**		

Country	ODA (mn $)	% GDP	% Social Investment
Aid Dependent			
Lao P.D.R.	141	19.9	0.0
Zambia	388	18.0	7.8
Ctl. African R.	189	17.5	9.6
Lesotho	118	17.1	13.0
Dominica	22	16.9	10.5
Burundi	198	16.5	34.4
Benin	247	16.1	20.5
Nepal	488	15.5	8.3
Madagascar	320	15.4	4.3
Guinea	346	15.0	5.0
Togo	182	14.7	3.5
Burkina Faso	284	14.5	3.0
Senegal	652	14.4	8.5
Bhutan	40	13.3	29.3
St. Vincent	17	13.1	0.0
Ethiopia	702	12.2	18.1
St. Kitts	14	11.7	64.3
Kenya	967	11.6	20.7
Rwanda	238	11.5	5.3
Papua N.G.	334	11.4	2.7
Zaire	637	11.1	18.1
Bolivia	432	11.0	19.9
Belize	29	11.0	8.7
Sierra Leone	99	10.6	8.8
Grenada	14	10.1	0.4
Subtotal	**7,098**		

Country	ODA (mn $)	% GDP	% Social Investment
Aid Influenced			
Jamaica	258	9.9	34.7
Bangladesh	1,791	9.8	5.6
Ghana	543	9.7	6.3
St. Lucia	21	9.5	-
Sudan	760	9.4	2.6
El Salvador	446	9.3	48.9
Uganda	397	8.9	20.7
Haiti	198	8.8	13.6
Botswana	162	8.4	68.7
Nicaragua	227	8.1	6.2
Sri Lanka	558	7.9	38.3
Lebanon	132	7.8	11.3
Jordan	280	6.3	10.4
Honduras	256	6.2	28.5
Liberia	58	5.9	7.8
Swaziland	29	5.0	-
Subtotal	**6,116**		

Total	**16,950**		
ODA Total	**34,120**	**1.3**	**15.2**

Source: *Human Development Report* (1991), T. 18.

Table 5.5

World Bank Countries: ODA & DFI, 1989 (US $mn)

WB No.	Country	ODA*	Percent GNP	Remittances	Percent ODA	Net DFI	Percent ODA
	Highly Aid Dependent						
I	Mozambique	759	59.2	-	-	0	0.0
4	Somalia	440	38.9	-	-	-	-
3	Tanzania	918	32.0	0	0.0	0	0.0
32	Lesotho	118	26.0	-	-	13	11.0
7	Malawi	394	24.9	-	-	-	-
9	Chad	239	23.5	(21)	-8.8	(12)	-5.0
16	Mali	470	22.6	39	8.3	(3)	-0.6
6	Lao P.D.R.	141	22.5	0	0.0	-	-
	Subtotal	**3,479**		**18**		**(2)**	
	Aid Dependent						
34	Mauritania	195	19.4	4	2.1	3	1.5
10	Burundi	198	18.6	-	-	I	0.5
26	Ctl. African R.	189	17.1	(29)	-15.3	-	-
8	Nepal	488	16.0	0	0.0	0	0.0
25	Benin	247	14.7	57	23.1	I	0.4
17	Niger	296	14.5	(40)	-13.5	18	6.1
42	Angola	140	14.4	-	-	200	142.9
45	Senegal	652	14.0	30	4.6	(20)	-3.1
28	Togo	182	13.6	4	2.2	-	-
12	Madagascar	320	12.6	(11)	-3.4	6	1.9
30	Guinea	346	12.6	0	0.0	10	-
23	Kenya	967	11.7	(3)	-0.3	69	7.1
2	Ethiopia	702	11.6	-	-	-	-
18	Burkina Faso	284	11.1	147	51.8	2	0.7
19	Rwanda	238	11.0	(17)	-7.1	16	6.7
11	Sierra Leone	99	10.5	0	0.0	-	-
27	Ghana	543	10.3	3	0.6	15	2.8
	Subtotal	**6,086**		**145**		**321**	
	Aid Influenced						
43	Bolivia	432	9.6	(1)	-0.2	(25)	-5.8
52	Papua N.G.	334	9.5	46	13.8	186	55.7
4	Bangladesh	1,791	8.9	771	43.0	0	0.0
14	Uganda	397	8.4	-	-	0	0.0
29	Zambia	388	8.3	(21)	-5.4	-	-
31	Sri Lanka	558	7.9	338	60.6	27	4.8
62	El Salvador	446	7.6	242	54.3	0	0.0
15	Zaire	637	6.6	-	-	12	1.9
65	Jamaica	258	6.6	71	27.5	28	10.9
68	Botswana	162	6.5	-	-	129	79.6
69	Jordan	280	6.3	561	200.4	0	0.0
53	Honduras	256	5.2	-	-	37	14.5
	Subtotal	**5,939**		**2,007**		**394**	

Table 5.5 continued

World Bank Countries: ODA & DFI, 1989 (US $mn)

WB No.	Country	ODA*	Percent GNP	Remittances	Percent ODA	Net DFI	Percent ODA
	Aid Recipient						
44	Egypt	1,578	4.7	4,254	269.6	1,586	100.5
47	Zimbabwe	266	4.5	-	-	(9)	-3.4
49	Cote d'Ivoire	409	4.4	0	0.0	n.a.	-
72	Costa Rica	224	4.3	-	-	115	51.3
57	Cameroon	470	4.2	3	0.6	31	6.6
55	Congo P.R.	91	4.0	(55)	-60.4	0	0.0
89	Gabon	134	3.9	(151)	-112.7	80	59.7
54	Guatemala	256	3.1	40	15.6	80	31.3
24	Pakistan	1,119	2.8	1,902	170.0	170	15.2
74	Mauritius	57	2.7	-	-	26	45.6
103	Israel	1,192	2.6	-	-	-	-
66	Tunisia	247	2.5	482	195.1	24	9.7
60	Namibia	44	2.3	-	-	-	-
61	Paraguay	91	2.2	-	-	21	23.1
50	Dominican R.	141	2.1	306	-	110	78.0
51	Morocco	443	2.0	1,325	299.1	167	37.7
33	Indonesia	1,830	1.9	125	6.8	735	40.2
48	Philippines	831	1.9	360	43.3	482	58.0
59	Ecuador	162	1.6	-	-	80	49.4
56	Syria	139	1.2	225	161.9	-	-
13	Nigeria	339	1.1	(19)	-5.6	2,082	614.2
64	Thailand	697	1.0	-	-	1,650	236.7
58	Peru	300	1.0	-	-	59	19.7
20	India	1,874	0.7	2,650	141.4	425	22.7
21	China	2,227	0.5	138	6.2	1,400	2.6
87	Uruguay	38	0.5	-	-	1	2.6
76	Argentina	215	0.4	0	0.0	1,028	478.1
77	Malaysia	139	0.4	-	-	1,846	1328.1
70	Panama	17	0.4	-	-	12	70.6
78	Algeria	153	0.3	355	232.0	(59)	-38.6
67	Turkey	122	0.2	3,040	2491.8	663	543.4
63	Colombia	62	0.2	459	740.3	546	880.6
71	Chile	62	0.2	-	-	259	417.7
90	Iran	89	0.1	-	-	-	-
88	Yugoslavia	43	0.1	(151)	-351.2	-	-
91	Trinidad	6	0.1	0	0.0	36	600.0
85	Brazil	189	0.0	-	-	782	413.8
75	Mexico	97	0.0	321	330.9	2,241	2310.3
83	Venezuela	21	0.0	(368)	-1752.4	77	366.7
	Subtotal	**15,161**		**11,585**		**9,314**	

Table 5.5 continued
World Bank Countries: ODA & DFI, 1989 (US $mn)

WB No.	Country	ODA*	Percent GNP	Remittances	Percent ODA	Net DFI	Percent ODA
	Other						
40	Sudan	760	-	297	39.1	0	0.0
82	Nicaragua	227	-	-	-	-	-
39	Myanmar	220	-	0	0.0	154	70.0
41	Viet Nam	138	-	-	-	-	-
80	Lebanon	132	-	-	-	-	-
35	Afghanistan	95	-	-	-	-	-
38	Liberia	58	-	51	87.9	-	-
36	Bhutan	40	-	-	-	-	-
37	Kampuchea	25	-	-	-	-	-
	Subtotal	**1,695**		**348**		**154**	
	TOTAL	**32,360**		**14,103**		**10,181**	

Source: *World Development Report* (1991).

Part Two

THE WORLD BANK:
MARKET- OR PEOPLE-FRIENDLY?

Ruben P. Mendez

Of the many reports issued by public international organizations, the World Bank's *World Development Report* is probably the most widely read. Its data are broad-ranging, timely and extensively used. There are, of course, other more detailed reports, such as the *World Debt Tables,* OECD's *Development Co-operation Report* and the IMF's *International Financial Statistics.* But these are for specialized audiences and purposes, and the *WDR* is probably the best single report for a general compilation of data on development. Its publication each May is therefore a special occasion, to which both development practitioners and academicians look forward. It is a time when they can review the latest data and update themselves.

The views expressed in this paper are those of the author and do not necessarily reflect those of UNDP. Part of the paper is based on a book by the author, *International Public Finance: A New Perspective on Global Relations* (NewYork: Oxford University Press, 1992).

The World Bank also uses the occasion of the publication of the *WDR* to expound a special theme. In 1988 the Report focused on public finance, in 1989 on financial systems, in 1990 on poverty, and in 1992 on the timely subject of the environment. The categorical free-market views of the World Bank permeate all of these expositions. In the case of the 1991 Report, the subject of the colloquium convened by the Lester Pearson Institute for International Development, the virtues of the marketplace constitute the special theme of the Report.

The objectivity of the World Bank's statistics does not characterize its thematic expositions, which are ideologically based. These expositions, however, are presented tendentiously and with the same magisterial stance as the statistical section. In view of the large readership of the *WDR*, the convening of this colloquium to discuss the 1991 issue in depth is a salutary undertaking. There is a need to reassure the world that economic theories - whether Communist or capitalist - cannot be ideologically decreed nor presented as dogma.

In his opening presentation, the 1991 *WDR*'s principal author, Vinod Thomas, gave an inspired overview of the report, i.e. of its expository part, and of its main concerns. There were four important points I particularly noted:

a) that development assistance has worked, as demonstrated, among other things, by a doubling of living standards and a halving of infant mortality rates in recent years;

b) that there is a need for a reduction of trade barriers by the industrialized countries, and for increased support to developing countries in the form of financing and assistance in policy reform;

c) that growth is a prerequisite for development: we should aim at "unbridled" growth, while targeting the problems of poverty and the environment;

d) that developing countries, for their part, should be more "market friendly," get prices and macroeconomic policy "right" promote competition, improve the climate for private enterprises, and deregulate.

With points a) to c) I am in general agreement, although what constitutes policy "reform" is arguable. I was favourably impressed by Mr. Thomas's defence of the impact of development and his emphasis on "unbridled growth", combined with a pro-active targeting of the problems of poverty and the environment. While he did not go into the specifics of how this can be done, it does point to an important fact: there can be no development or poverty alleviation in the poor countries of the world without economic growth; complete redistribution and perfect distribution in a country where per capita income is only $200 annually will not go into the root of its problems. The problems are not simply how the pie is divided but how to have a larger and complete welfare pie. For all of these, development assistance is needed, as is a recognition by the industrialized world that its trade restrictions are a serious constraint to the growth of the developing countries.

I am not so sanguine, on the other hand, about the *WDR*'s diagnoses and all-encompassing prescriptions concerning development policies and activities, which are encapsulated in the term "market friendly". Nor do I agree with the *WDR*'s statements that there is a consensus on this view, and that it has been born out by experience. This is a view from the North, or at least from Bretton Woods, rather than a universal view.

I was recently discussing the concept of "market friendliness" with Paul Streeten, who remarked that the market is a mechanism, and what development policy should seek to be is "people friendly". The description of the Macintosh as "user friendly", it will be recalled, refers to persons and not to mechanisms. While development has many facets, this indeed should be the guiding philosophy of development. Being "people friendly" is, in the final analysis, the true meaning of "human development".

There have already been excellent critiques of the *WDR* by Paul Bowles, Barry Lesser and Tony Tillett (not to mention the detailed technical analysis by Lance Taylor with his colleagues at MIT, José María Fanelli and Roberto Frenkel). The panellists and other participants have also raised important questions in the course of the discussions. They have questioned, for instance, whether competition *per se* is always desirable since it does not deal with the environment. The United States may wish to ensure that tuna fishing companies do not deplete marine resources or trap dolphins with the fish, and this may lessen their competitiveness vis-à-vis others not as environmentally concerned. They have also noted that markets do not address the problem of poverty. The observation about Julius Nyrere's role in Tanzania as being nation-building and not only socialism was also discerning. In these days of ethnic strife in Africa, Asia and Europe, one can appreciate the value of long-term effectiveness as well of efficiency.

Among the 1991 *WDR*'s principal shortcomings is its cavalier dismissal of the problem of market failures. Its discussion of market failure is rather brief:

> It was assumed that in the early stages of development markets could not be relied upon, and that the state would be able to direct the development process. The major development institutions supported these views with varying degrees of enthusiasm. By the early 1980s the dominant paradigm had shifted (p. 33).

While private enterprise competition is in many respects an efficient mechanism for allocating resources, it continues to be subject to market failures, both nationally and internationally. These include an inability to produce public goods, to deal with externalities (both positive and negative, the latter of which are at the root of problems of the environment) and to prevent competitive breakdowns. Although the subject of such failures is not as widely or as intensely articulated as the virtues of the marketplace, the fact is that it cannot be ignored by policy makers and scholars, and is an area in which the public sector has to give a helping hand. A judicious mix of free markets and public sector intervention is necessary. With the almost total demise of communism, it is the mixed economy that is now more than ever the dominant system as well as the dominant paradigm.

The following are some of the market's main shortcomings:

a)   It is unable to ensure the production of public goods or their production at adequate levels. The reason for this is that for most public goods, people cannot be excluded from consuming them, and there is no additional cost in the consumption of the goods by an additional person. Private enterprise, therefore, will find no motive for producing them since it cannot earn a profit from doing so. Thus, clean air, highways, police protection - and at the international level the maintenance of the ozone layer, peacekeeping and the prevention of marine pollution - all need intervention by the public sector.

b) It is incapable of dealing with negative externalities. Private firms by themselves will not take into account the costs of environmental pollution, nor the tensions caused by the arms race, since these costs are not reflected in their income-and-expenditure statements or balance sheets. These costs, while "external" to the firms, are very real, and the intervention of the public sector, say through taxes, regulation and fines, is necessary to internalize them so that they are reflected in the cost accounts of their producers.

c) It is unable to capture as financial returns for the producers the external benefits of certain goods, which will therefore be underproduced by private firms in a completely free economy. One example is education, which benefits not only the person receiving the training but also society at large. Another example is the prevention and control of communicable diseases. Benefits are not only to the recipients of vaccinations but also to others, because there are fewer carriers and transmitters of disease. If left to the market mechanism, such external benefits will be underproduced because private producers do not capture the full returns. This is why various education and health programmes are publicly subsidized.

d) It cannot cope with competitive breakdowns, such as monopolies and monopsonies, incomplete markets and information. Incomplete markets include the lack of markets for capital and credit. The underprovision by the private sector of capital to the less developed countries is a *raison d'être* of public institutions such as the World Bank. Even the IMF may be considered as filling in for another market failure - the lack of insurance for countries experiencing severe balance of payments difficulties as a result of exogenous events (even though the IMF acts as though the difficulties were due to mismanagement and not outside factors).

Although strictly speaking not a "market failure", the market also does not address the question of poverty alleviation and distributional equity. Economic efficiency is not concerned with the problems of poverty and the extremes of income and wealth. A "people friendly" economy thus calls for public sector intervention.

Another shortcoming of the *WDR*'s approach, which is incorporated in the World Bank's structural adjustment programmes, is the fallacy of composition: that what is good for one is good for all. This applies, among other things, to devaluations, which the World Bank insists upon to make countries more competitive in the world market. For instance, Kenya may be forced to devalue its currency to make its tea exports less expensive overseas, which could have an adverse impact on another tea exporter, Sri Lanka. If Sri Lanka were forced to do the same the effects of these actions would cancel each other out, with the tea-importing countries (not the least the United Kingdom and the United States!) benefiting.

Despite protestations to the contrary, the IMF and the World Bank seem to have a standard recipe, based on assumptions that market failures are less important than government failures, that the rational allocation of existing resources is more important for growth than increasing resources or at least a pre-condition for it, that "getting prices right" is the highest priority, and the like. Critics ask for greater or more balanced emphasis on market failures compared to government failures, for supportive infrastructure as well as price incentives, for symmetrical adjustments by creditor countries, and for more sensitivity to the dangers of competitive devaluation by debtor countries.

It would have been useful for the *WDR* to have empirical studies to illustrate its thesis on the effectiveness of its SAL and other development policies. Existing studies on SALs are highly critical. A detailed analysis by Mosley, Harrigan, and Toye,[1] including nine case studies, states that in very poor countries, the Bank's policies have been a "gratuitous obstruction", where privatization and the removal of infant-industry protective structures are "at best an irrelevance". The analysis concludes that while SALs have generally been favourable to export growth and the external account, they have almost everywhere also depressed aggregate investment and had a neutral effect on national income, financial flows from overseas and distribution. They have "consisted of a mixture of protection for the inefficient, intervention with a social rationale (e.g., food subsidies)", indicating that "there are more justifications for government intervention than the Bank has generally been prepared to accept and ... further work to determine the appropriate form and levels of such intervention is now urgent".

A study by UNCTAD[2] covering twelve least developed countries that carried out IMF-negotiated structural adjustment programmes indicates that their performance did not differ significantly from that of least developed countries as a whole. The lack of any consistent relationship between the adoption of structural adjustment programmes and economic performance, as reflected in growth, the current account balance, and inflation brings these programmes into question. The foregoing, plus the high social costs of these programmes and the political instability they produce, make one wonder whether the World Bank and the IMF fully understand the consequences and implications of their policies.

There are alternatives to the present laissez-faire pattern of North-South resource flows. This pattern consists almost entirely of official development assistance (ODA), which is almost completely voluntary, non-concessional public sector loans and private investment - all of which, everyone in the colloquium agreed, have been inadequate and do not have bright prospects for substantial improvement. Among the alternatives, which are discussed in detail in a recent book I have written,[3] are the following:

a)　The global commons can be the subject both of user charges and regulation for environmental purposes. A precedent may be found in charges for the exploitation of the deep ocean bed, which has been designated part of the common heritage of mankind by the United Nations Convention on the Law of the Sea. Similar policies can be applied to navigation and overflight, Antarctica (a disputed common) and the Southern Ocean, the geostationary orbit and the electromagnetic spectrum.

b)　There are possibilities for true international taxation, both for revenue-generating and corrective, or "Pigovian", purposes to internalize negative externalities. Such taxes are ubiquitous in national systems of public finance. Internationally - aside from the assessed financial obligations of member states to the regular budgets of the United Nations and its traditional specialized agencies and quota subscriptions to the IMF and the World Bank - precedents may be found in the Montreal Protocol on Substances that Deplete the Ozone Layer, and in the European Community. In the latter, members of the Community pay 1 percent of their value-added-tax (VAT) income to the European Commission - a form of an international revenue tax - with the percentage increasing gradually over the years as Europe-wide legislation supersedes national legislation. The potentials deserve serious consideration. The volume of international trade in 1989 amounted to $3,140 billion in 1989, as measured by the volume of imports, so that a tax of only 0.1 percent could have yielded over $3 billion.

c)   Other possibilities that could be revisited are the proposed Special Drawing Right (SDR) - and gold-development links.

    i)   Although the IMF's Articles of Agreement state that SDRs, sometimes called "paper gold," shall become the principal reserve asset, the IMF has not issued any since the last allocation of 1979-81, on the grounds that there does not appear to be a shortage of world liquidity. While this may be true of the industrialized countries, it is not the case with the developing countries, which are very much in need of foreign reserves to pay for their imports and their debt burden. A new issuance of SDRs plus their distribution, at least in part, on the basis of need, could go a long way in resolving the world's debt crisis and the need for capital for development.

    ii)   The IMF still has 103 million ounces of gold in its coffers. If these were sold - again, in line with a standing agreement, that gold should be phased out in the international monetary system - the proceeds could be used for development purposes. If the IMF sold less than half of its gold stock, say 50 million ounces, over a period of time at an average price of $350 per ounce, the proceeds would amount to $17.5 billion. A precedent exists in the IMF's sale of part of its gold holdings in the late 1970s, allocating part of the proceeds to a trust fund for concessional loans to developing countries.

Despite warnings by the delegates to the IMF of the United States, Germany and other rich countries, scientific models and other computations by respected economists show that SDR - and gold-development links would not be inflationary.

There is much that remains to be done and can be done to promote development in the poor countries and the world at large. While the market can be harnessed to help in this process, we cannot afford to be blind to its limits. The end of the cold war should not be seen as the triumph of the market over the state. It should be seen, rather, as an end to extremism and a time to develop new means of financing, focusing on the well-being of the people.

[I found the meeting highly useful. As I have drawn to the attention of my senior colleagues at UNDP, I believe it would be beneficial for UNDP staff to participate more frequently in discussions with economists and other development specialists from universities and other organizations in colloquia such as the one organized by Tony Tillett. The process of cross-fertilization would be valuable both in increasing the awareness by UNDP staff of current economic thinking and by other organizations of the work that UNDP is doing in the development field, both operationally and intellectually.]

NOTES

[1] Mosley, Paul, Jane Harrigan and John Toye, *Aid and Power: The World Bank and Policy-Based Lending,* 2 vols. (London: Routledge, 1991).

[2] United Nations Conference on Trade and Development, *Trade and Development Report 1989* (New York: United Nations, 1989).

[3] Mendez, Ruben P, *International Public Finance: A New Perspective on Global Relations, op. cit.*

PROGRESSIVE CAPITALISM

Robert Miller

As the seminar demonstrated, there are two quite different reactions to the 1991 World Development Report. Some see it as a profoundly conservative document because it makes a strong case for the role of the market in economic development. Others, myself included, think it comparatively progressive because it points out that the market cannot do everything. It finds that some challenges of development, like helping the poorest people, must be met by strong effective, government.

In the present ideological climate, that amounts to boldness. The defeat of communism has been seized upon by the libertarian right to show that government does not and cannot work, from which it follows that the less of it the better. Skilful propaganda mixed with the deeply cynical mood of many people in the industrialized democracies converted this bit of ideology into folk wisdom. Today, those who have a good word to say for government have become a timid minority, afraid to appear in public during daylight hours.

In these circumstances, it is all the more surprising that the 1991 World Development Report (the broadsheet of international capitalism, as some see it) has a good word to say for government. Generally speaking, what it says is that governments should leave the production and distribution of goods and services to the market while recognizing that there are many other tasks at which markets prove inadequate or fail altogether.

> That is why governments must, for example, invest in infra-structure and provide essential services to the poor. It is not a question of the state or market: each has a large and irreplace-able role.

There you have it: the World Bank has said that there is a large and irreplaceable role for government. The Report labels its overall approach to development as "market friendly" although, given the political winds blowing these days, it might have been more helpful to call it government friendly or, better still, people friendly. In most parts of the world, it is not markets which are under assault but governments, or rather the notion that governments have something useful to contribute to human welfare.

There is another very sensible and important thing the 1991 Report has to say, namely that the first element of a market friendly approach is investing in people. The Report points out that the economic returns - the *economic* returns - from public and private investments in people are often extremely high and that these particular investments are the special responsibility of government:

> Markets in developing countries cannot generally be relied upon to provide people - especially the poorest - with adequate education (especially primary education) health care, nutrition and family planning services.

This amounts to a revolution in the vocabulary of political discourse. Investment in people? We have been trained in the belief that education and health care and the rest are social or welfare programs, good or bad for the soul depending on your point of view, but certainly not a hard-headed investment. But here comes the

World Bank saying that investment in people is an important element.

All of this strikes me as quite progressive capitalism. It is a much needed corrective to the right wing bunk that has been parading as political wisdom for most of the past decade. It is a reminder that the late nineteenth and the earlier twentieth centuries applied a corrective to capitalism - the corrective of countervailing government power - without which it might well have suffered the same fate as communism. (Not that the corrective was much appreciated by capitalists at the time, or since. Franklin Roosevelt was fond of saying that it was his job to "save the bastards from themselves.")

The World Bank Report has a good word to say for government but it is less charitable about particular governments. The 1991 Report finds that third world governments spend too much (time and money) doing what they should not do (playing around with their economies) and not nearly enough investing in people. It calls for increases in both the quantity and quality of these investments noting, for example, the advantages of primary health care systems over expensive curative systems. What is particularly appealing about that bit of advice, and much of the rest, is that it applies as well to developed as to developing countries. Just to catch the attention of the Bank's largest shareholder, the Report mentions that "by some estimates Shanghai has a lower infant mortality rate and longer life expectancy than New York City."

The only problem with this advice - a problem associated with the entire thrust of the 1991 Report - is that it has been around for a long time and generally ignored. The World Bank is too sanguine about the happy complementarity of the market and government. The notion that capitalists will maximize their profits while governments satisfy basic human needs amount to the last gasp of yuppie economics: yes indeed, the Bank seems to be saying, you *can* have it all! Unfortunately the historical record cited by the Bank suggests otherwise.

If investment in people, particularly the poorest, is the best investment, why do so many countries under-invest in people, especially the poorest? The answer is as plain as the nose on your face - power. What is missing from this Report, and from every World Bank Report, is the element of political power. Although it may be economically and morally compelling to invest in people, the decision to do so depends on influence over government. And while there may be societies in which the poor are powerful, they are few and far between. This problem explains why the progressivism of the 1991 World Bank Report is so unconvincing in the end. In the wake of the Los Angeles riots, it reads too much like the good intentions that pave the road to hell.

The story of Los Angeles offers a less hopeful picture of the future than does the World Bank, although it may be more consistent with the political facts of life. The picture is of an increasingly polarized and ghetto-ized world in which the upper and middle classes insulate themselves to the extent they can against the intrusions of mass poverty. An observer of the riots explained the logic behind this future: "It is cheaper to clean up one of these messes every twenty years than it is to correct the problems." If that is the logic of the north, who believes that the much poorer south will accept the advice of the World Bank?

MARKETS, STATE AND TECHNOLOGY

Amitav Rath

The seminar organized by the Lester Pearson Institute for International Development to critically review the World Development Report (1991) (WDR) is a valuable initiative. WDR (1991) is a specially pertinent document as it is an ambitious attempt to review the development experiences of the past decades, often going back three to four decades, and at times much further, to examine the economic growth experiences of the early industrializers. The ability of The World Bank to marshall financial resources and experts, the skills and knowledge of its large staff, and, its own experience of financing economic development for over forty years, all combine to provide the report an intellectual weight which cannot be easily duplicated by any other institution. When this is combined with the facts that the views of the Bank are expected to be reflected in its own lending policies, the largest single source of financial flows for most poor countries, that these views also influence the policies and frameworks of other bilateral, multilateral and private financial institutions, and thereby, necessarily set the policy framework available to the borrowing states, they add substantial practical weight to the intellectual. So the value of this seminar, to critically review the "Challenges of Development" which have been identified by the Bank, are obvious. In fact, the importance of this report suggests it deserves greater sustained and careful response than what I can provide at this brief workshop.

Given the limitations of time and space I can only address a few selected issues. This requires choices to be made on the issues to focus on. The difficulties in making the choices are obvious when one notes that the report was generated by a team of over twenty World Bank experts, assisted by consultants, and, is laid out in 180 pages of carefully written text, 41 boxes which highlight specific questions and experiences, 30 tables and 35 figures which support the text, and an additional 33 tables covering important development data on over 100 countries. It is precisely because of the amount of information and the quality of analysis that the WDR is always eagerly awaited by students and practitioners of development.

My task is made somewhat easier by the excellent reviews already carried out by Barry Lesser and Tony Tillett of Dalhousie University, and Paul Bowles of Saint Mary's University, and the fact that a number of commentators such as Ruben Mendez are touching on some aspects of the report. These circumstances, I believe, allow me to be somewhat idiosyncratic and organize my comments in three parts, grouped around things I liked, things I did not like, and some suggestions for the future. I take a look at the report from the perspective of the literature on technical change.

First, I wish to congratulate Mr. Vinod Thomas and his team for their selection of the themes which are taken up in the WDR as they are of fundamental importance. I believe the team has to be congratulated for its attempt to take a look at *all* the important factors which contribute to development and the fact that development is not collapsed into the single dimension of GNP or even economic growth, though the primary focus is on economic issues. I believe the team also must be congratulated for being able to adopt a relatively pragmatic and empirical approach to the issues (though I am less convinced on how successfully they have managed to stay consistently with the approach when drawing certain policy conclusions and recommendations and will discuss these later). Finally, I must say that I was positively impressed by the inclusion by the team of a number of insights from studies of technological change, their impact on economic growth and development, the factors which seem to affect technological change positively and negatively, and, how policies can help improve the contribution of technology to the removal of poverty.

I am in almost complete agreement with the broad conclusion reached in the overview:

> (Development) is not a question of intervention versus laissez-faire - a popular dichotomy, but a false one. Competitive markets are the best way yet for efficiently organizing the production and distribution of goods and services. Domestic and external competition provide the incentive that unleash entrepreneurship and technological progress. But markets cannot operate in a vacuum - they require a legal and regulatory framework that only governments can provide. And, at many other tasks, markets prove inadequate or fail altogether...It is not a question of state or market: each has a large and irreplaceable role (p. 1).

This is a statement that appears almost "revolutionary" in a decade dominated by the nostrums of Reagan, Bush and Thatcher who argued that the State is always a hinderance and a withering away of the State was a necessary condition for economic growth. It is almost a revolutionary statement for finance ministers in many poor countries who have had to dismantle the state under the pressures of external and domestic deficits and the resultant Structural Adjustment Programmes designed and supported by the Bank and external donors.

There are many other useful statements and conclusions in the report. The historical review of thinking on development, pointing out that it "has repeatedly shifted over the past forty years," "progress has not been along a straight line," and the attempt" to gleam from the evidence, the accumulated knowledge and insight" are all very salutary and should (p. 4) encourage humility and receptivity to new ideas. Such a framework supports approaches which are more open, and, less ideological and dogmatic.

The report does not ignore issues which are not strictly economic such as military spending, wars and political instability on development (p. 2). Nor does it ignore issues which are external to individual developing countries and therefore beyond their influence, but nevertheless have a major, if not dominant, impact on the success or failure of national policy. The Bank highlights the non-tariff trade barriers imposed by Industrial Countries which range from 42% of total trade for Japan to a high of 55% for the EC (p. 104). It estimates the annual loss of DCs from these export barriers to be over 50 billion dollars and points out that this is larger than the concessional financial flows to the DCs. It also points out that large deficits in the Industrialized Countries (ICs) raise interest rates, reduce resources available to the developing countries and to the extent IC policies lead to recessions and economic instability, they negatively affect the opportunities for growth in the DCs.

Finally, the report does a commendable job of reviewing a number of key issues in technology and economic developments. Some of the points are integrated through the text and a number receive special attention in Chapter 5. Here the discussions cover the different channels of technology transfer, point out the needs for domestic technological capacity and the need to support innovation. It argues that DC governments need to pay greater attention to building technological capacity through more and better education, fostering competition, and developing a range of technology support institutions for information, quality, standards and so on.

Yet, while the report is in many ways an important contribution to the consideration and articulation of the knowledge acquired from past experiences spanning several decades, it also falls short of its own goals in several ways. My main criticisms are that in several places attempts are made to marshall empirical evidence in a "scientifically" rigorous fashion in support of the views advocated by the Bank but which remain quite unsatisfactory.

Second, within the report evidence contradictory to the position adopted by the Bank are presented but then dismissed as not being relevant.

Third, many times the conclusion states that there is a need for a joint role between the state and the market, but with little elaboration of how the state can in practice play those roles, given other recommendations which reduce its resources, policy options and capacity for implementation.

Finally, the report can be criticised for the framework within which it is articulated, and for what is not discussed, the evidence not cited, the issues which are not raised as in the case of the famous dog which sometimes did not bark. I will provide a few examples of the above.

In marshalling its statistical evidence, the Bank finds (on pp. 5, 47) that over 22 years, between 1965-1987, countries with high education grew at the highest rates, those at the other extreme grew more slowly, and those which had one and not the other were in between. In an ecumenical spirit, the report raises questions on measurement (p. 44), "there are serious gaps in data on literacy, school enrolment," "GDP measures pose important problems in comparability across countries and over time," "PPPs generally yield a more accurate measure of output," "Policy conclusions based on analysis of meagre data sets can be seriously biased." I would also add a final question, that even when strong association is found between two variables, we have to decide which is the cause and which the effect or whether they both may be the effects of a separate causal variable. In the above example, we have no idea of how many and which countries fell into the three categories; was education and distribution measured at the beginning of the period, the end of the period or was an average taken over the 22 years; was GDP used for the analysis or PPP; how robust was the country classification to the chosen and to alternate measures, as many other different statistical measures suggest themselves; and why is "distortion" measured as the foreign exchange premium grouped differently in Figure 5; Table 2.4; and Figures 4.1 and 4.2. Finally, in all these analyses of "distortion" and its effects on economic growth, the question is not raised as to whether a possible explanation is that *other* factors promoted economic growth, which in turn allowed or enabled policies of low distortion and high education. Which is the cause and which the effect?

Having "established" that the "few economies which had relatively undistorted prices did well"(p. 4), it goes on to ask the important question "why did the interventions in East Asia lead to success and not failure?" It answers that it was because they (the

East Asian States) were "disciplined," "competent," "pragmatic" and "flexible." This conclusion does not sit well with its earlier conclusion on the role of the State. The Bank may well counter that "appropriate" interventions by a "competent" government together with a careful use of the market could be optimal, but in the absence of such a "competent" state, markets are better than incompetent *dirigisme*. But it never actually comes out and states it in so many words.

There are many examples of incompetent governments and of inappropriate interventions documented in the report which have been counter productive. But all examples of misapplied and ineffective interventions do not prove that interventions *per se* are bad or not required. The case for non-intervention rests ultimately not on empirical evidence but on the premises of neoclassical economics, on the efficiency of markets and the efficiency and completeness of the set of market prices in their information content, for the rational actions of economic agents. In spite of the attention paid to technology in the report, the entire paradigm of the report remains uninfluenced by arguments and constructs raised by economists who have focused on issues of technical change and innovation. Newer concepts of economic theory, such as those emphasizing learning and evolutionary processes in economics, the fundamental uncertainty of the future, the role of expectations and the existence of nonlinearities and a number of inherent instabilities of the system, have no room in the framework. In these new formulations, markets are given a critical role as in the neoclassical, but a different one. In such a revised framework, an increasing role of markets, in fact, also includes and requires an increased role for an activist, interventionist state, not a state which retreats from the economy and only redresses market failures.

It is the lack of such a revised framework which makes the Bank report unable to deal with contradictions between certain evidence, some of it cited in the report and its recommendations. Two good examples of such contradictions are the discussion of the issues regarding state intervention in trade (p. 102) and on commodity price movements (p. 106). My own conclusions from the Bank's own statements in the report of the case for or against state intervention lead toward state intervention and that the Bank's own data on commodity price movements supports The Prebish-Singer hypothesis. But, it is impossible for the report to acknowledge this without undermining its overall thesis. So the same data suggests the opposite conclusion for the Bank.

In marshalling its case for freer trade, the Bank presents data on tariff rates by the early industrialisers. First, the data presented supports a view that tariffs were lowered by countries *after* they achieved a certain industrial level. Second, its does not even discuss the non-tariff barriers which were also used in the past. Finally, in concluding that presently industrialized countries did not take recourse to very high tariffs, it ignores the much higher transaction costs to international trade in the past leading to effectively higher barriers to international trade.

One final example of the problems resulting from inappropriate frameworks is found in the conclusions from Table 2.3, that, during 1960 to 1973 and to 1987, TFP for East Asia grew most rapidly and so supports market oriented policies. South Asia had lower TFP growth rates in the same period due to protectionist policies. Another conclusion possible is that the data, in fact, supports the role of intervention. Perhaps, in the case of South Asia, the earlier decade of high capital investment led to a second decade of high TFP growth. Or again, when the report examines the development experience of countries (pp. 38-39) its consistent line is that market oriented reforms at a particular point led to higher growth rates. But, for many of the same countries, the periodization may well be wrong. A longer historical periodization could well argue a first period which combined low state intervention, insertion into the global markets and low growth; followed by an interventionist state which made structural changes to the economy, leading to higher growth; and only then followed by a liberalization, which led to even higher growth.

There are many, many other examples which can be provided where one can argue with the evidence cited and not cited, the conclusions reached and the policies recommended. This can be an amusing or challenging intellectual exercise if it was not for the importance of the views of the Bank on the lives and future possibilities of many. Its importance requires us all, individuals, professionals, and the institutions, in this case The World Bank and Dalhousie

University to examine how we can make this process of critical review and "learning" from the development experience more efficient and more effective in guiding better policies. For if we recommend to developing countries that they unilaterally open themselves to free trade regimes, even if the rich do not, we minimize the possibility that after a few years, we do not conclude it was all a mistake. Mistakes cannot be avoided and certainly as we improve our knowledge, some of our current building blocks will be discarded, but we must endeavour to minimize mistakes and their impact on the poor.

A first step towards improving our "learning" has been taken by the Bank team in its attempt to distil the experiences from development practice together with a framework of economic theory. Necessarily, the views from the Bank will be influenced by the chosen theoretical perspectives, the data available and also by the political, sociological and historical experiences and context of the institution.

This should necessarily be challenged by alternate perspectives, other evidence and other interests. This is a necessary process to continually improve and refine our approximations of the "truth." It is in such a process that we have been engaged, and the Lester Pearson Institute for International Development and the World Bank must be congratulated for their roles in initiating and participating in it. What is required, is to strengthen this process and to build upon it. Further steps in this direction are urgently required. To take it further requires greater time and resources than we can devote at this seminar; it requires institutions such as the Lester Pearson Institute to engage in it on a longer term, and on a sustained basis. It also requires that the Bank and other development agencies provide both the resources and improved processes for this search for "knowledge" and "truth" so that they will be more efficient, effective and "risk averse" in policy recommendations.

AN OPEN LETTER TO MR. VINOD THOMAS, CHIEF ECONOMIST OF THE WORLD BANK

Dear Mr. Thomas:

We, as concerned people, believe that the period we are living in is crucial in determining the future of our planet. In the midst of tremendous political restructuring, which has bolstered the hand of traditional strategies of economic development, the environment around us deteriorates, peoples struggle to retain their cultural values, and the numbers of poor continues to grow each day.

These problems require careful consideration and in some cases radical change in our attitudes towards what constitutes development. The path shown by industrialized countries cannot be duplicated because of the strain on natural resources it would imply, not to mention limitations on consumer spending. The model also seems flawed at a human scale, as a resurgence of racism and prejudice is seen throughout the industrialized world. If development policies are to resolve the problems of poverty, cultural destruction and environmental degradation, the application of traditional strategies of economic development is not sufficient. Growth in GDP per capita is not a good measure to gauge development. What is needed is an approach which equally integrates concerns of human development, cultural diversity and environment. While the Bank shows some signs of recognizing an integrated approach, the dominance of Structural Adjustment Policies reverses any positive trends.

Simply opening developing countries to forces of the international marketplace encourages the destruction of the domestic food and manufacturing industries and ensures industrialization on the basis of low wages. Application of restrictive monetary policies induces a domestic recession which simultaneously reduces real wages and increases inflation due to the structure of consumption. SAPs have also prevented the upkeep of infrastructure facilities which permit the recurrence of diseases like cholera, produce a poorly educated nation and reduce economic activity. Moreover, the application of these policies is socially detrimental as evidenced by a long history of riots and government repression sparked by the implementation of SAPs.

There has been much talk lately about a redemocratization of the developing countries and linking this process to structural adjustment. One can seriously question the existence of democracy in the international sphere when every time an elected government tries to implement policies designed to strengthen national control or the domestic economy, the international community acts to destabilize and ostracize this country. The examples of Chile in the early 1970s, and Peru and Nicaragua in the 1980s, emphasize this point. The international version of democracy seems to mean that every country is free to implement structural adjustment policies and nothing else. The World Bank has played a key role in winning the battle of ideologies, but the losers have always been the people, indigenous cultures and the environment.

If real democracy is to exist, the international community must respect the desire of all people to choose and implement alternative economic and political structures. Each time the people of developing countries are denied these opportunities, the repercussions that will one day surface becomes all the more serious. It may not happen in your life time Mr. Thomas, but you know it will. Similarly, if all problems such as the debt crisis, environmental deterioration and protectionism are all resolved through imposition by the industrialized nations, these resolutions will be unsustainable.

The role of the World Bank will be vital in determining the course of development. If real solutions to the problems of developing countries are to be found, the World Bank must shed off all ideological blinders and ensure that a balance be found in respect to social, political and economic concerns. It must become the voice of reason rather than dogma.

The World Bank must creatively seek to resolve the debt crisis. It must encourage the stimulation of domestically oriented production in developing countries and work with elected governments to implement policies on which they were empowered to implement. Finally, the World Bank must work to protect the environment and cultural diversity, the two things which truly make our world a beautiful place to live.

Thank you.

LPI COLLOQUIUM:

THE WORLD DEVELOPMENT REPORT (1991):
THE CHALLENGE OF DEVELOPMENT

March 27 & 28, 1992, Dalhousie University

Background

The Lester Pearson Institute for International Development (LPI) is convening a meeting to examine the most recent *World Development Report (1991): The Challenge of Development*. The report, published last year, summarizes the lessons of past development thinking by the World Bank Group, and sets out a number of research and policy proposals for the decade ahead. The principal recommendations are for more market orientated policies, open economies, an appropriate macro-economic environment and a commitment to human resource developmet. The Bank intends this volume to set the course of development thinking (both at the Bank and elsewhere) for the immediate future.

The LPI Colloquium will examine the assumptions and conclusions of the World Development Report and consider its value to researchers and development agencies (with particular reference to Canada) as a blueprint for development action in the years ahead.

Structure

The meeting is intended to raise questions, examine issues and provide a forum for discussion of development in the coming decade. The structure of the meeting is intended to reflect this commitment to discussion and dialogue. Hence, while individual participants may be asked to be particularly prepared to contribute to certain sessions, there will be no "formal" papers presented, other than an "issues" paper for each session, which sets out some questions for initial discussion.

Three themes (covering three principal sessions) have been identified to provide the basic content structure for the colloquium. These are:

1) Does development theory determine or rationalize practice?

An examination of the role of theory as a reactive and proactive force in the past and its challenges for the present and future, remembering Schumpeter's dictum that "Economic theory is always at least ten years behind the economy."

2) International agencies and national states: dialogue for development?

The session will discuss the international context within which the World Bank and developing countries policy dialogue takes place, and the extent to which the outcomes of these exchanges promote development.

3) Does development assistance matter?

A consideration of aid and reform as instruments of change with application to Canada's ODA policy - are they complements or substitutes? How can they be made complementary if they are not already?

Organization

Each of the three main sessions (one for each theme) will be organized as follows:

- a chair who will responsible for guiding audience participation and bringing the discussions to a sensible end;

- an introduction by a person responsible for a review of main issues at the commencement of each session and a summary at the end of the session;

- a number of participants who will be expected (primed) to discuss particular issues of thinking about development issues;

- audience participation and debate of the issues.

Participants

A number of participants have been invited from outside the region. They are:

Pierre Beemans, Director General, Corporate Affairs & Initiatives Division, International Development Research Centre (IDRC)

Jim Carruthers, Director, Policy & Planning, Asia Branch, Canadian International Development Agency (CIDA)

Don McMaster, Director General, Canadian Partnership Branch, Canadian International Development Agency (CIDA)

Ruben Mendez, Chief, Technical Support Division, UN Sudano-Sahelian Office, United Nations Development Programme (UNDP)

Robert Miller, Parliamentary Centre

Amitav Rath, Policy Research International, Ottawa

Vinod Thomas, Chief Economist, Asia Region, World Bank, and principal author of the World Development Report (1991)

Other Colloquium participants will be drawn from faculty and graduate students. A complete list will be provided prior to the meeting.

Background Papers

Apart from the World Development Report (1991) itself, the participants responsible for introducing the different subject areas will identify the key issues for the sessions to follow; these short papers will be available at the commencement of the colloquium.

Venue

The Seminar Lounge, Main Floor, Henson College of Public Affairs and Continuing Education, Dalhousie University, 1600 University Avenue, Halifax, Nova Scotia.

Timetable

Friday, March 27

12:00   Buffet Lunch for visitors - Lester Pearson Institute

14:00   Session 1 - Introduction
            Keynote Statement: The Challenge of Development -
            A review of the WDR (1991): Vinod Thomas
            Session Topic: Does development theory determine or
            rationalize practice?

17:00   End of Session

19:30   Dinner - Great Hall, University Club
            Speaker: Elisabeth Mann Borgese -
            "Reflections on development challenges for the 1990s"

Saturday, March 28

9:00   Session 2 - International agencies and national states:
            dialogue for development?

12:00   End of Session

12:15   Lunch - Great Hall, University Club

13:30   Session 3 - Does development assistance matter?

16:30   Wrap-up

17:00   End